Nature Thought of It First

Text by Lucy Berman   Illustrations by Roy Coombs

GROSSET & DUNLAP
Publishers · New York

Published in 1972 in the United States
by Grosset & Dunlap, Inc., New York.
All rights reserved.

Library of Congress Catalog Card Number: 79-166189

ISBN: 0-448-02089-0 (Trade Edition)
ISBN: 0-448-03166-3 (Library Edition)

Printed in Holland by N.O.I., Amsterdam.

Contents

Introduction

There is so much to discover about the lives of plants and animals that every day new wonders are revealed by people who are inquiring into nature's ways. How do animals see and hear? How do they navigate during journeys that cover thousands of miles? How do they find their prey and escape their enemies? The answers to all these questions are fascinating—and they are also very useful to man. For nature is a great innovator, a solver of problems. She has provided the bat with an exploration system that enables it to navigate in total darkness. To the glowworm she has given a signal lamp to use in locating others of its kind.

Many human inventions are based upon the same broad principles as nature's devices. Some, such as the webbed "duck's-foot" flippers that skin-divers wear, have been copied directly from nature. Others, such as radar systems for locating objects, have been developed independently by man, and separate research has revealed their parallels in the natural world.

Man began imitating nature in primitive times. The Greek myths tell the story of a boy named Perdix, who was very ingenious and clever with his hands. Thomas Bulfinch, the American writer who retold the Greek myths in simple English, described how Perdix came by the idea for one of his inventions: "Walking on the seashore he picked up the spine of a fish. Imitating it, he took a piece of iron and notched it on the edge, and thus invented the *saw*."

The story of Perdix is a myth, but the imitation of nature is very much a reality. Scientists today are devoting much of their time and thought to probing nature's secrets. They have discovered how to manufacture the chemicals that some insects use to attract their mates. With these artificial attractants they can lure insect pests into specially-prepared traps and destroy them completely.

All kinds of interesting devices have been proposed by modern biologists. They include an artificial "dog's nose" that could be used for tracking down criminals, and a robot car based on the principle of the frog's eye, which sees only light and darkness, edges and moving objects.

This is a book about some of the things that nature thought of first; and also about some of the man-made devices that have duplicated what animals and plants do naturally. I hope that it will encourage you to read further, and learn more of the amazing beauty and ingenuity of the living world.

Camouflage and Disguise

Most visitors to the zoo enjoy looking at the big cats, admiring them for their strength and beauty. They see the handsomeness of the striped tiger and the spotted leopard, often wondering whether these lovely patterned skins are of any use to the animals themselves. When a leopard is moving about in a bare cage, it is difficult for an observer to imagine the possible benefits of a spotted coat. If the zoo visitor could see the leopard in its natural habitat, however, he would understand that this apparently conspicuous animal is actually hidden by its dazzling spots.

In a tale called "How the Leopard Got His Spots," Rudyard Kipling gives a delightful explanation of the value of the leopard's markings:

"Now you *are* a beauty . . . You can lie out on the bare ground and look like a heap of pebbles. You can lie out on the naked rocks and look like a piece of pudding stone. You can lie out on a leafy branch and look like sunshine sifting through the leaves; and you can lie right across the center of a path and look like nothing in particular. Think of that and purr!"

The effect of the leopard's spots, the tiger's stripes and many other natural skin-patterns is to camouflage the animal by making it appear to merge completely into the back-

The chameleon can change its color—to blend with its surroundings—in fifteen minutes.

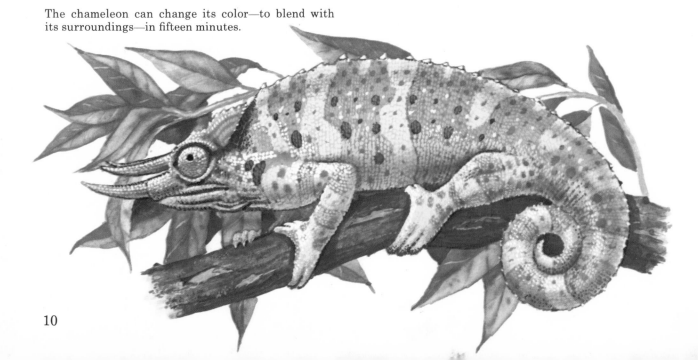

A tiger is camouflaged in the long grass and remains invisible to its prey. Man also uses camouflage in order not to be noticed, especially when at war. This Spitfire, used in the Second World War, is painted in colors that mingle with the ground colors, making it unnoticeable from the air.

ground. A tiger walking through tall dry grasses blends perfectly with their yellow stems and black shadows. A speckled, sandy-colored flatfish is virtually invisible as it lies on the sandy bottom of the sea. Similarly, such insects as the geometrid moth and the white spotted moth are so patterned that they can scarcely be distinguished from the branches they rest on. The eye is so fooled by this patterning that the outline of the animal is not apparent. When you cannot see the shape of the animal, you are unlikely to see it at all. The advantages of such camouflage are obvious: the animal remains invisible both to enemies and to possible victims.

Another good method of camouflage is color harmony. Some animals can change color so that they match the color of their surroundings. Among these animals are several species of spiders, called flower-spiders. The spiders crouch inside similarly-colored flowers, waiting for insects to come within their reach. A canary-yellow flower-spider placed on a white flower can fade to white in less than a week. If the white spider is then removed from the white flower and put back on a yellow one, it soon begins to change again to yellow. The most expert natural color-change artist is a lizard called the chameleon. A brown chameleon put among green leaves will turn bright green

in only fifteen minutes. The spider, the chameleon, and other talented "colorists" such as prawns and cuttlefish, change color by reflex action. Light-sensitive cells beneath the skin register the light-intensity of the animal's surroundings. Signals are transmitted to the brain, which then sends instructions to layers of pigment cells, causing them to spread along the surface of the skin and create a particular color effect.

There are many other methods of camouflage which include the use of distinctive shapes, as well as colors and patterns.

Flatfish change color to match the seabed. It is probably the eye of the fish that is the light-sensitive organ controlling the change, for blind fish do not change.

Two remarkable camouflaged fish are the Sargassum fish, which lives in the weed-filled Sargasso Sea, and the Australian seahorse. Both these fish are so well disguised that when they are swimming amid patches of seaweed they completely "disappear."

Men at war have been quick to learn the benefits of camouflage, and have designed combat clothing with patterns that blend into jungle scenery. Camouflage artists have also applied these techniques to disguising buildings, by painting them so that the outline of the building is difficult to discern.

Soldiers fighting in the jungle sometimes cover their helmets with leaves. The leaves disguise the helmet, and when the soldier crouches down among grass and bushes, he may easily escape being seen. Boats, machines, and stores of ammunition can also be concealed under leaves and branches, so that they are difficult to see from the air.

Covering oneself up so as to merge with the scenery may seem like a particularly human kind of cleverness, but similar tricks are played by such animals as crabs and insects. Many of these creatures do not try to hide themselves completely, but rather they disguise themselves as something else in the hope that if they are seen they will be ignored.

Spider crabs are very selective about the kind of camouflage they use. The spider crab gets its name from its resemblance to a spider.

Soldiers fighting in the jungle often disguise their helmets by covering them with leaves.

Below, left: A treehopper known as the thorn bug looks exactly like a large rose thorn. On the stems of a rose bush, treehoppers are completely disguised, even to the sharp eyes of birds.

Its body is small, and its legs are long and delicate. It moves fairly slowly, and a good disguise is a very useful protection from its enemies. Spider crabs cover themselves with bits of seaweed which they hang from spiny projections on their backs and legs. If a spider crab dressed in green seaweed moves to a bed of red seaweed, it will take off its green camouflage and exchange it for red. If it finds itself in a sponge bed, it will tear up bits of sponge and dress itself in these.

The young of an insect called the caddis fly build very well-camouflaged portable homes. A young caddis fly is a soft, wormlike creature that lives underwater. It weaves a tube-shaped home for itself out of silk, and then covers the tube with bits of stone or gravel, pieces of twig, leaves, and tiny shells. The insect stays inside the tube with its head showing beyond the opening. As it moves slowly through the water, it looks more like a harmless collection of rubbish than an insect.

Many animals do not need to cover themselves with camouflaging materials. Their

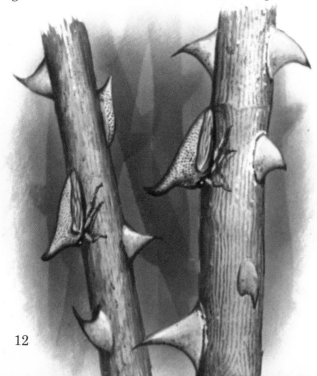

Top, left: The caddis fly larva weaves itself a silk tube-shaped home and then covers it with bits of gravel, twigs and leaves. As it moves slowly through the water it looks more like a harmless collection of rubbish than an insect.

Left: The Sargassum fish is so well disguised that it almost disappears in the seaweed of the Sargasso Sea.

Above: The spider crab is a true master of disguise, dressing itself in the very material of its surroundings. If a spider crab dressed in green seaweed moves into a patch of red seaweed it changes its green weeds for red.

Below: The geometrid moth is difficult to see against tree bark, not only because it is the same color, but also because the bands on its wings break up its shape.

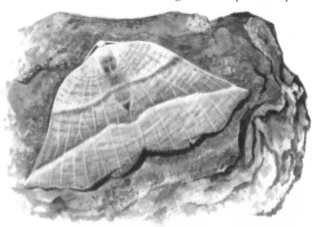

Below: The stink bug looks exactly like a piece of tree bark because of its color and texture.

natural appearance blends so well with their surroundings that as long as they remain still, they are nearly undetectable. Some animals rely on the color or pattern of their skins for disguise. The elaborate camouflage, not only of color and markings, but of shape, size and texture, may so combine that the animal looks exactly like a leaf or a twig.

The most dramatic examples of total disguise are found among insects. Stick insects are very long, slender insects that look exactly like sticks. Their thin legs are like leaf veins, and their heads are so small that they are scarcely noticeable. Stick insects move and feed during the night. In the daytime, they remain in an almost trance-like state, clinging motionless to the stems of plants. Another insect that copies a twig is the looper caterpillar, whose disguise gives it protection from insect-eating birds. There are insects that resemble leaves, such as the dead leaf butterfly of India, and others that look like tree bark, such as the stink bug, and like thorns, such as the Brazilian thorn bug.

13

Armor

One of nature's curiosities is a small mammal called the armadillo. The name armadillo comes from Spanish and means "the little armed one." This is beautifully descriptive of the animal itself, for the armadillo is as well-protected as a miniature tank. Its back is covered with an almost impenetrable armor, consisting of a layer of close-fitting bony plates. Some species of armadillo completely enclose themselves in their armor when they are attacked. They do this by rolling themselves up into a tight ball, leaving no soft or vulnerable part of the body exposed.

The armadillo is only one of a legion of strangely armored creatures. Natural armor takes many and varied forms, from the pointed quills of the porcupine to the crocodile's tough, leathery scales. All insects are covered by an outer shell or membrane,

Although the armadillo's name means "little armed one," its armor is not really as impenetrable as that of the medieval knight. It is made of small plates of bone, covered by a layer of horny skin. These plates are connected by skin from which a few hairs grow. The nine-banded armadillo (right) is common in Central America and Southern United States. The three-banded armadillo (far right) is the only armadillo that rolls up into a completely armored ball. The two triangles are its head and tail.

The pangolin (below) also rolls itself into a ball, and its name is as descriptive as the armadillo's: *peng-goling* in Malay means "the roller." Its overlapping scales, tough though they are, are really compressed hair.

Below: A more commonly seen armor is the shell of the turtle and the tortoise, who present a horny back to an enemy after pulling in the head and limbs.

Stegosaurus was a plant-eater that developed a strange and bony defense against meat-eaters. Its impressive armor did not save it from extinction.

composed of a strong material called chitin. In some insects, this membrane is exceptionally hard. Certain weevils, in particular, have an outer shell so strong that even a man cannot break it, except by giving the insect a sharp blow with a hammer. Such an armored shell enables an insect to withstand fairly vigorous pecking by insect-eating birds.

There are many bizarre species of armored fish. Some wear almost complete "suits" of bony armor, while others are equipped only with "helmets" of bone covering their heads, or with ridges of bone protecting various parts of their bodies. Among the oddest of the fully-protected fish are the blowfish. When these fish are frightened, they inflate themselves by taking in air or water, so that they look like blown-up balloons. Their skin is covered with bony thorns, and when the fish inflate themselves, these thorns stand erect, making the blowfish a prickly mouthful for its enemies.

Reptiles of various kinds are extremely well-armored. Turtles and tortoises resist attack by drawing the head and all four limbs within the shelter of their thick, horny shells. The turtle has two protective shells, an upper and a lower one. The upper shell, called the carapace, is thicker and stronger than the lower. All reptiles have scaly skins. The crocodile and its close relation, the alligator, have the toughest of reptile hides, but many fierce-looking, dragonlike lizards are also well-protected.

The most thoroughly armored of all reptiles have been extinct for millions of years. These were certain dinosaurs, or "terrible lizards," which died out some seventy million years ago. Most of the armor belonged to plant-eating dinosaurs, and was apparently developed as a defensive weapon against the ferocious meat-eating types. *Stegosaurus* was a fearful-looking plant-eater, with a double row of bony plates, shaped rather like primitive ax-heads, running the entire length of its spine. *Triceratops* was another well-armored creature, its huge head protected by three horns as well as a solid bony frill.

Human armor, on the other hand, is far from extinct. Although modern fighting men no longer wear the type of chain mail and heavy body armor worn by medieval knights, they do wear flak-suits or bulletproof clothing made from plastic or lightweight metal. Armored vehicles are also common, and include tanks, armored cruisers, and heavy armored cars designed for use by police and the armed forces.

The blowfish looks like an ordinary fish until it is alarmed: then it pumps itself full of water, and little spines project all over its body.

New Clothes

A garter snake sheds its old skin in one piece, emerging with glistening new scales.

Below: A weasel adapted to northern climates changes its coat in winter to match the snow. It molts again in spring, growing brown as the days grow longer.

Animals do not wear clothing as we do. You will not see a bear shopping for a new fur coat. Animals are clothed, however, in the sense that they are covered with protective layers of fur, feathers, scales and so on. These are not artificial garments, but are part of the animal's body, developing naturally as their owner grows. You may think that these protective layers are unchanging—a fixed sort of skin that always looks the same. But animal garments undergo many changes, and because of these changes they have more in common with human dress than you might suppose. Animals change their clothing from season to season, growing heavier coats for winter and sometimes changing the color to match the seasonal landscape. The weasel and the Arctic fox, for example, grow white coats to help them blend with the snow, and the ptarmigan

Top: The male scarlet tanager in his breeding plumage is indeed scarlet. But after his fine feathers have attracted a mate, he molts and resembles the female.

In winter the ptarmigan blends with the snow (above), and in summer (below) it blends with the rocks.

and willow grouse also dress in winter white.

Some animals undergo a complete or partial molt—that is, they discard one set of feathers, scales or fur for another. Molting may allow the animal to accommodate itself to seasonal changes. It may also occur because the old "garment" is worn out and needs replacing, or because the animal has outgrown its present covering—just as a child outgrows his clothes and must have new ones in order to avoid "bursting out at the seams."

All birds molt, shedding their early or "baby" plumage as they develop into adults, and also regularly replacing feathers that have become frayed and worn. Adult songbirds, and some others, molt every year, beginning just after the close of the breeding season. These birds do not shed all their feathers at once, since this would leave them unable to fly. Instead, each species has a set pattern of molting, which leaves them at some disadvantage but not completely unprotected. The most helpless of molting birds are ducks, geese and swans. Unlike other flying birds, these three varieties lose their flight feathers all at the same time, and are grounded until the new feathers grow in.

Certain birds undergo a change in fashion when they molt. The male bird grows bright, handsome plumage which he retains until the breeding season is over. Then, after he has succeeded in attracting the female with his fine feathers, he sheds them in favor of a more conservative style of dress.

Birds and mammals are not the only creatures that molt. Snakes and lizards shed their skins periodically. Most lizards shed their skins in patches, but all snakes and a few lizards cast off their old skins in a single operation. Spiders also make a complete molt when their old skins become too tight. A split develops in the skin along the edge of the spider's body, and the creature slowly withdraws its long legs from their old covering, as if it were withdrawing fingers from a glove. Like spiders, insects are also encased in a hard outer shell, and they must molt several times in order to grow.

17

Perfumes

For many living things, reproduction depends on a male and a female of the species uniting. Such meetings are generally made easier by the ability of the male and female to locate and to recognize one another. To ensure a fairly high reproduction rate, there is usually some way by which creatures can attract members of the opposite sex. Nature has provided many methods, including displays of brilliant plumage, special sounds or mating calls, and distinctive perfumes.

Perfumes are very useful as attractants. A few molecules of scent can travel for miles in the air, farther than any audible or visible signal. Also, perfumes are comparatively safe to use. An animal can give off perfume without moving or making a noise that might alert its enemies. It may even exude a scent so specialized that only members of the same species can detect it. In such a case, the animal can broadcast its signals in complete safety, with no possiblity of drawing a predator instead of a mate.

Plants attract bees and other insects by their perfumes in order to pollinate other plants of the same species: the insect gets its nectar and at the same time is dusted with pollen which will be deposited in the female part of another blossom. The scent of the cuckoo pint (above) is repulsive to humans, but flies can't resist it.

Many mammals have special scent glands which produce attractant perfumes. Dogs, rabbits, foxes, deer and numerous other animals have strong-smelling scents which help members of the opposite sex to locate them and which keep members of the same sex from intruding on each other's territory. The scent is deposited as droplets of fluid, on bushes or tree branches, or on the ground. This fluid is very long-lasting, and may continue to give off an identifiable odor for several weeks. This enables animals which roam over long distances to discover one another's movements, despite a considerable lapse of time.

Certain insects rely entirely on attractant perfumes in their search for a mate. Chief among these are various moths, particularly the silkworm and emperor moths. The female silkworm moth releases a few molecules of a substance which to humans smells faintly and pleasantly of leather. This odor draws the male moth like a magnet to the female's side. Male silkworm moths have been known to fly as far as seven miles in response to the female's scent signal. The male is able to smell the female's perfume at this distance because he has a "special nose" for her odor. Certain cells on his delicate antennae are capable of responding to that scent alone, and to no other in the world. Consequently, the male is never confused by the presence of a great many other scents in the air around him.

Plants also use attractant perfumes, but in a less direct way than animals do. The male and female elements of plants cannot travel under their own power to meet each other. Therefore, the plant uses perfumes in order to attract insects to it. As the insects fly from flower to flower, they carry the pollen grains —the plant's male element—and deposit them, either in the same plant or another plant, where they can penetrate down to the ovary, which contains the ovules, or female element of the plant.

Human beings, like animals, have their own natural attractant odors. They also use a variety of manufactured scents in order to make themselves more attractive. Some of these are derived from plant and some from animal sources; others are synthetic. They may not work as effectively as the perfume of the female silkworm moth, but they are very pleasant anyway.

Male silkworm moths have been known to fly as far as seven miles in response to the scent signal of the female.

The feelers of the male Luna moth look like tiny yellow ferns, but are really antennae with a highly developed sense of smell. The sole function: to catch the scent of the female.

The concentrated musk of the civet is offensive to humans, but when it is diluted it is pleasant enough to be used in the most expensive perfumes. In Africa civets are sometimes kept in captivity so that the musk can be removed from their glands several times a week.

The alligator snapping-turtle opens its huge jaws to reveal the bait: a small red growth on its tongue. A fish, lured into the jaws by this wormlike object, is immediately snapped up and swallowed.

Man uses the same principle to catch a fish, and has invented a tremendous variety of lures to put on the end of his fishing line.

Lures

Any fisherman will tell you that it takes cunning to catch a fish. You cannot just dangle a plain steel hook in the water. Fish must be tempted to bite, by a nice juicy worm or a piece of bright, flashing metal. The worm is an obvious attraction, since fish are usually hungry and will snap at anything that looks edible. The reason why some fish attack shining objects is less certain. It may be because such metal lures look like small injured fish, swimming unsteadily and showing brief glimpses of their silver underbellies.

Fishermen take advantage of hungry fish, by offering a carefully chosen bait to attract them. But humans are not the only ones to use this clever ploy. A group of fish called angler fish use ingenious dummy baits to lure their unsuspecting prey. The first ray of the angler fish's back fin forms a sort of fishing-rod with a wormlike or balloonlike lure on the end. The angler fish dangles this lure invitingly in front of its open mouth. Smaller, greedy fish swim eagerly toward the bait, and as soon as they come within reach, the successful angler fish seizes them in its huge, needle-sharp teeth.

There are various species of angler fish. Some which live in the dark depths of the Atlantic Ocean are equipped with a luminescent bait resembling a shining marine worm. One type of angler, the fishing frog, pulls its worm-like bait into its mouth as the prey approaches. This trick is very similar to what

a man may do when he is catching crabs: he dangles his bait at the end of a string which he reels in slowly, so that the crab, following the moving bait, swims straight into the fisherman's net.

Not all fish which go fishing for their food are equipped with fishing rods. The Western Stargazer, which belongs to a different group from the angler fish, simply extends a deceptive little "worm" from the inside of its lower lip. The Stargazer lies partially buried on the sea bottom, so that its unwary prey sees nothing but what appears to be an unprotected meal.

Lures provide a very lazy way of getting food, and there are other creatures, besides fish and human beings, who use them. The alligator snapping-turtle sits with its huge jaws open wide, twitching a red-spotted area

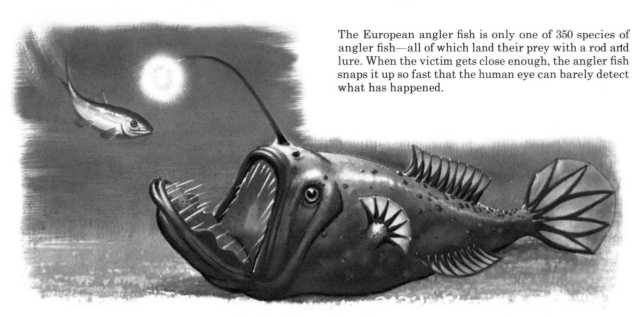

The European angler fish is only one of 350 species of angler fish—all of which land their prey with a rod and lure. When the victim gets close enough, the angler fish snaps it up so fast that the human eye can barely detect what has happened.

at the tip of its tongue. This serves as a lure for worm-eating fish, who quickly find themselves trapped and eaten.

A remarkable and very attractive lure is employed by an African insect called the devil's flower. This insect, which is a type of praying mantis, uses its resemblance to a flower in order to draw flies and other insects to their death. Hanging upside-down from a twig, the pretty red and green mantis waits comfortably for some curious fly to attempt to alight upon it. With lightning speed, it grips the fly in its strong pincers and devours it.

While the mantis attracts other insects by its resemblance to a flower, the equally

The decoy: a hunter attracts wild ducks with wooden ones. The *Ophrys* orchid (right) attracts a wasp with a blossom that looks like another wasp.

interesting *Ophrys* orchids make themselves alluring to insects by means of a structure resembling a female insect. The orchids do not harm their visitors, but use their contact as a means of spreading pollen from flower to flower. The technique of attraction is much like that of a duck hunter, who uses decoy ducks to lure live ones.

The devil's flower (below, right) is really a mantis, but attracts insects because it looks like a flower.

21

Traps

Everyone knows that animals eat plants, but did you know that some plants eat animals? It may sound a little like a horror story, but there are actually several hundred species of insect-eating plants. Scientists believe that these plants eat insects in order to obtain the nitrogen that is lacking in the soil where they grow. The plants digest their food by dissolving it in powerful acid liquids, very similar to the digestive juices found in humans and other animals.

Before they can begin the process of digestion, however, the plants must first catch their "dinners." Since insects move very swiftly, and plants are firmly rooted, the plant must set some sort of trap for its victim. Insect-eating plants are equipped with various kinds of traps, some of which operate much like the traps that humans use to catch insects and animals.

The leaves of some insect-eating plants are covered with a sticky substance. When an insect alights upon such a leaf, it sticks fast, just as a fly becomes stuck to a piece of flypaper. The insect is not powerful enough to free itself from the gummy mass, and the harder it struggles, the faster it sticks.

Plant traps that are coated with natural "glue" often have other mechanisms as well which they use to secure their prey. A little

marsh plant called the sundew has leaves covered with reddish, hairlike tentacles. At the end of each tentacle is a drop of sticky fluid that sparkles like dew in the sun. Flies and other insects are attracted to this sparkling surface, and come to rest upon the leaf. They end up sticking to the gummy

The shiny, sticky tentacles of the sundew (below, left) attract an insect, trap it, wrap around it and push it toward the center of the leaf where it will be digested. The pitcher plant (below) lures victims to their doom in a similar way. Nectar at the rim of the plant attracts the insect, which then topples into the "pitcher" and drowns. Man has yet to develop a better way of trapping insects; a glass of diluted molasses is one of the best ways he has of dealing with a plague of flies or wasps.

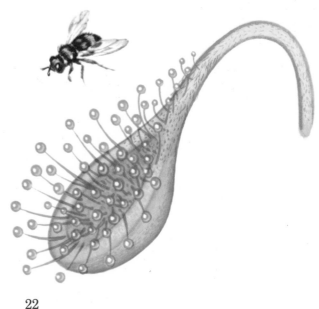

The classic insectivorous plant is the Venus's flytrap. Even a grasshopper can be taken in by the sweet stickiness; then the leaf of the plant snaps shut and the insect is trapped by the teeth. Several days later, when every edible part of the insect has been digested, the leaf opens again.

A mouse, about to be trapped by one of the oldest tricks in nature's book—even though it is a man-made trap.

tentacles. But this is not the entire trap; the plant has further surprises in store. Almost at once, a tentacle begins to curl around the insect's body. When it is wrapped completely around, it begins to push the captive toward another tentacle, nearer the center of the leaf. Meanwhile, glands in the leaf pour forth an acid liquid which, within minutes, starts to dissolve and digest the insect.

Much of what we know about the sundew was first described about a century ago by the great English naturalist, Charles Darwin. Darwin, whose theories on evolution completely changed men's ideas about the history of life on Earth, was fascinated by insect-eating plants. After years of study, he wrote a book, published in 1875, called *Insectivorous Plants* ("insectivorous" means insect-eating). He described the sundews and also

the pitcher plants. These have pitcher-shaped leaves which contain digestive liquids. Insects are attracted to these leaves by colors or odors, and, once inside the pitcher, are unable to climb out. Eventually they drown. A molasses trap—a jar containing molasses and water—is a simple device for catching insects that is very much like the pitcher plant.

Of all the plants that Darwin studied, there was one, the Venus's flytrap, that he called "the most wonderful plant in the world." The Venus's flytrap works rather like a steel-jawed animal trap. Its leaves bristle with half-inch-long teeth along their edges. On the inner surfaces of the leaves are sensitive trigger hairs. When an insect touches these hairs, the two halves of the leaf close up, the teeth interlock, and the insect is securely trapped inside.

The pit trap is a very old device for trapping large animals, such as the rhinoceros. A deep pit is dug, and then grass and leaves are laid over the top to disguise it. The unsuspecting animal falls in and—if the pit is deep enough—cannot get out.

Pit Traps

In a famous children's story called *Winnie-the-Pooh*, the English author A. A. Milne described a most unusual animal trap. Pooh, who often spoke of himself as "a bear of very little brain," had decided to catch his version of an elephant—the Heffalump—and he explained his plan to his friend Piglet:

"'Piglet, I have decided to catch a Heffalump. . . . I shall do it,' said Pooh, after waiting a little, 'by means of a trap. And it must be a Cunning Trap, so you will have to help me, Piglet.'

"Pooh's first idea was that they should dig a Very Deep Pit, and then the Heffalump would come along and fall into the Pit . . . the Heffalump might be walking along, humming a little song and looking up at the sky, wondering if it would rain, and so he wouldn't see the Very Deep Pit until he was halfway down, when it would be too late."

Winnie-the-Pooh may have been a bear of very little brain, but his plan for catching the Heffalump was really quite practical. Men have been using pits to catch animals since prehistoric times. Usually, their traps have been even more "cunning" than Pooh's, in that they have cleverly concealed the opening of the pit with a cover of branches and leaves. Such a covered pit, known as a pitfall, can trap even an animal that does not have its head in the clouds as it walks along.

Men are not the only users of pit traps, however. Other animals besides Pooh have constructed very clever pit traps for capturing their prey. These animals usually lie in wait at the bottom of the trap, and thus combine trapping with the techniques of ambush so common in Western films.

One creature which builds a Very Deep Pit, indeed, considering its size, is the ant lion. The adult ant lion is a graceful insect resembling a small dragonfly. The young or larvae of the ant lion are fat and wingless, with flat heads and short, stumpy legs. The adult lives a very short time and does not eat, but the larvae eat as many insects as they can trap. An ant lion larva uses its shovel-like head to dig a funnel-shaped hole in dry sand.

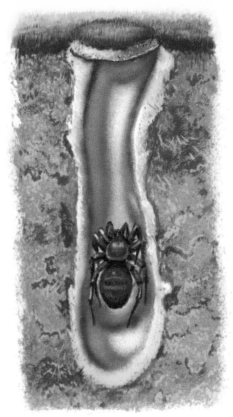

The trapdoor spider digs a hole and sits near the top waiting for its supper. It holds its silk trapdoor slightly open until an insect is near, then flings open the door, grabs the insect and pulls it inside.

The larva of the tiger beetle digs itself a long, narrow tunnel and waits at the top, with its huge, flat head blocking the entrance. When an insect passes by, the beetle leaps backward and snares the victim in a surprise attack.

Below: The pits of the ant lion. The larvae wait at the bottom of their pit traps for unsuspecting insects to fall in. Any that do not fall in automatically are shot down with a blast of sand.

Then it digs itself deep into the sand at the bottom of the pit, so that only its head is showing. When an ant or other small insect steps over the edge, it slides down the side of the pit, while the ant lion hurls sand upward to prevent its prey's escape.

The tiger beetle is another cunning insect that lays an effective trap for its victims. The larva of the tiger beetle digs a narrow vertical burrow that may be more than a foot deep. It blocks the entrance to the burrow with its gigantic head, which is at a right angle to its body. As soon as an unsuspecting insect begins to walk over the trap, the beetle jumps up and seizes it in its powerful jaws.

Possibly the cleverest of all animal traps is that constructed by the trapdoor spider. This spider digs a hole in dry ground, and lines it with silk. It then makes a silken door which neatly covers the opening of the hole. The spider sits in the burrow, holding the door slightly open, and whenever it senses that an insect is near, it flings open the door, grabs its victim and drags it underground.

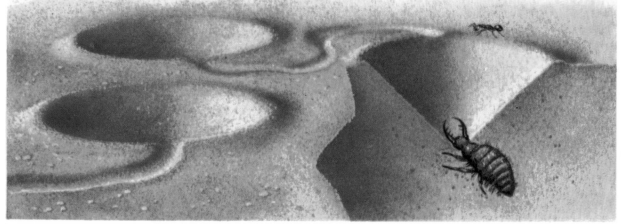

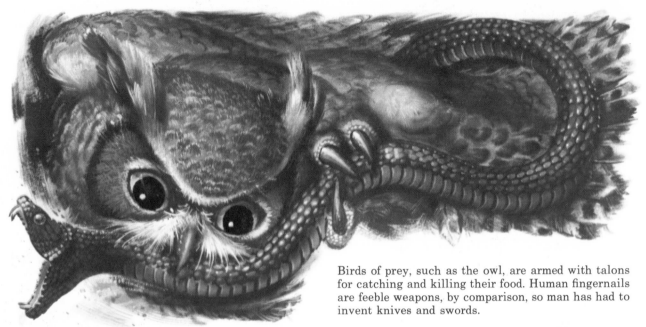

Birds of prey, such as the owl, are armed with talons for catching and killing their food. Human fingernails are feeble weapons, by comparison, so man has had to invent knives and swords.

Swords, Knives and Water Pistols

Animals need weapons of some sort simply to stay alive. If they are meat-eaters, they must be able to kill or at least stun their prey. Whatever they eat, they need some form of self-defense against other animals intent on eating *them*. Not all animals are equipped with offensive weapons. Some rely on protective coloring to camouflage them, or on various other devices. Among those animals that are "armed," however, knives, swords and even water pistols play useful roles.

Knifelike weapons are common among birds of prey. Such birds as owls, eagles, hawks and falcons have talons as sharp as needles. Many birds of prey strike with their armed feet as they fly, killing their victims on the wing.

Teeth and tusks can also be dangerous weapons. Ferocious meat-eaters, such as wolves, have four strong and extremely sharp fighting teeth called canines. The canines of a wolf are as effective as a butcher's knife in dealing with its prey. In some animals, the two upper canines are very long, and project outward from the animal's

mouth. Such teeth are called tusks. A heavy animal which lowers its head and charges into battle with tusks forward, can inflict wounds much more serious than those made by a charging man carrying a spear.

Sword-bearing animals have always fascinated men. There are many tales of the destruction wrought by swordfish upon fishing boats of all sizes. Swordfish normally use their weapons as broadswords, lashing them about from side to side, rather than attacking with the sword point forward. However, it is not surprising that a swordfish is capable of driving its head straight through the side of a boat. If a 600-pound swordfish,

Archer fish (above, left) gun down their insect prey with a natural water pistol. These sharpshooters can easily hit their target at a distance of six feet, and have been known to "spit" as far as fifteen feet. The pistol shrimp (above, right) is even more like a gunslinger, for it points a claw, aims, and fires a jet of water that stuns the victim. The swordfish uses its natural weapon like a broadsword, to stun its prey. But the sword is also useful for parting water and undoubtedly has something to do with the high speed of the swordfish.

swimming at about ten nautical miles an hour, collides head-on with any obstacle, it strikes with a force of as much as a third of a ton.

There are many more examples of cutting and piercing weapons in the animal world, too numerous to mention. The water pistol, a far more sophisticated device, is much rarer in nature. Most people have amused themselves with water pistols at some time. They are not really dangerous weapons, as far as we are concerned. The archer fish, by contrast, uses a natural water pistol to shoot insects out of the air so that they topple helplessly into the water. An archer fish shoots by closing its gill flaps, and forcing a pressurized jet of water through a tube formed by its tongue pressing up against a long slot in the roof of its mouth. With this watery ammunition, the archer fish can hit insects five or six feet above the surface of the water. It is a skill which improves with age: the older fish are the better marksmen.

Another pistol-slinger is the pistol shrimp. This shrimp ejects a jet of water through a groove in its claw. It actually points the claw like a pistol, and stuns its victim with the water jet. The vibrations from the shrimp's "firing" have been known to shatter the sides of thick glass containers.

When disturbed, a skunk will raise its tail and stamp its front paws as a warning, then turn its back and squirt a pungent fluid at its attacker. Its aim is always accurate, and sometimes temporarily blinding. Usually, however, the musky odor is enough to send the predator running in the opposite direction.

The caterpillar of a tussock moth is colorful, but its hair transmits a poison that can be very irritating.

Chemical Weapons

Men have developed many subtle and terrible weapons of war. Among the most dreadful, because of their effects on innocent people and whole landscapes, are chemical weapons. These include poisons and paralyzing nerve gases, blister gases which burn the skin, and various types of tear gases which cause irritation and itchiness. Man has practiced chemical warfare for many thousands of years. Poisoned arrows, still used by some savage tribes, are very ancient weapons in the human arsenal. Toxic fumes, causing "slumber and yawning," were used in battles in India as far back as 2000 B.C.

But animals have been employing chemical artillery for attack and defense for much longer than man. Reptiles, insects, fish and even a few mammals use poisons and harmful fluids against their enemies. Some of these animals inject strong, even deadly, poisons when they bite or sting. Others are equipped with special stinging cells which cause irritation or paralysis in any enemy that touches them. Certain mammals, notably the skunk, and other creatures discharge repulsive-smelling fluids or gases, usually in self-defense.

The best-known type of chemical fighter is the poisonous snake. Only about ten per cent of all snakes are harmful. But it is easy to understand the unpleasant reputation of snakes as a group when one considers that the venom of some snakes is so deadly that it kills in minutes. All venomous snakes produce their venom in special poison glands. From the glands, the poison flows to the fangs. These may be grooved, so that the poison runs down them as the snake bites, or they may be hollow, like a hypodermic needle. Snakes with hollow fangs inject their venom through the victim's skin. Most snake venoms contain combinations of two poisons, a nerve poison and a blood poison. Among the deadliest snakes are the copperhead, rattlesnake, fer-de-lance and bushmaster.

A great variety of chemical weapons are

Man has used chemical weapons for thousands of years. One of the most ancient is the blowgun, a long hollow tube through which poison darts were blown. Top: Cross-section of a rattlesnake's fang. The venom is carried by a hollow tube that runs from the venom sac to a small hole near the tip of the tooth.

Many octopus species are equipped with a poison that kills their prey, and the poison of the blue-ringed octopus is deadly to humans, as well.

found in the insect world. Bees, wasps, hornets and some ants possess poison-injecting stings. Certain caterpillars are covered with stiff, poisonous stinging-hairs. These break very easily when the caterpillar is touched. The broken ends can pierce the skin, and the poison they contain causes painful irritation.

Some ants which do not have stings secrete from their abdomens a strong-smelling acid called formic acid. This is produced in the ant's poison glands. A fighting ant may squirt acid at its enemies from a distance of up to ten or twelve inches. A tiny beetle, the acid-spraying bombardier beetle, also squirts acid from its tail end. This liquid explodes in the air to form a little cloud of "tear gas."

Scorpions and spiders, two close relatives of the insects, can often carry out fatal assaults on their foes. The scorpion uses its tail-sting to inject poison, while the spider bites and leaves poison in the wound.

Many types of fish are equipped with poisonous spines. Jellyfish possess microscopic stinging cells. The Portuguese man-of-war is a huge jellyfish whose stinging cells can cause numbness or even heart failure in humans unlucky enough to touch it.

The bombardier beetle is one of many beetles which are capable of discharging "tear gas." But in the case of the bombardier there is an audible "crack"—and there can be as many as twenty explosions in rapid succession. Chemicals stored near the tail of the bombardier are responsible for these explosions, and for the irritating vapor they produce. It is unpleasant enough to drive away even the largest predator.

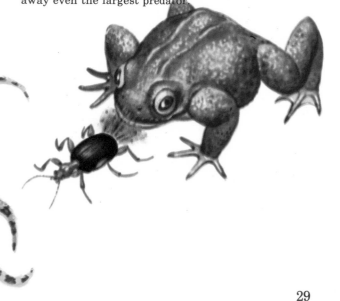

Wheels and Tracks

According to legend, there was once a snake that rolled along the ground like a hoop, carrying its tail in its mouth. No real snake has ever been known to travel this way, but there is one group of snakes, the sidewinders, whose motion is similar in principle to that of a wheel.

To understand this comparison, we must first understand the forces at work when a wheel moves forward along the ground. Imagine the circular wheel as being composed of a series of segments. As the wheel turns, only one of these segments touches the ground at any moment. For a tiny fraction of a second, the segment touching the ground is still; then it moves on and is replaced by a new segment. As each new segment touches the ground, it becomes a temporary stationary point, through which power is transmitted. The wheel segments push backward and downward, while the ground pushes upward against them. As each segment is lifted, the wheel moves around, and a new segment is brought into contact with the ground.

When the sidewinder moves, segments in two regions of its body are stationary and touching the ground at any given time. These segments push against the ground and receive an equal and opposite push from the ground. The remainder of the snake's body is lifted clear of the ground. As the snake progresses, it twists its body sideways, throwing a loop which extends to one side in front of its head. When segments are added to the stationary track, they are added from this loop. The snake's body unrolls as it moves until it can once more touch the ground with its head, and again form a loop. As it moves forward, looping its body from side to side, it leaves a series of parallel tracks on the ground. These tracks are perpendicular to the direction in which the snake is traveling.

A wheel has a single axis, around which it rotates, and this axis is perpendicular to the wheel's motion. Because the sidewinder cannot grip its tail in its mouth, and roll over the ground like a wheel, it cannot have a

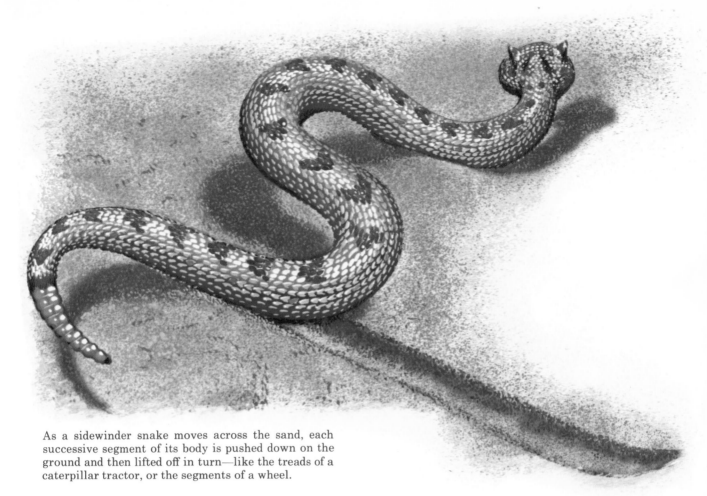

As a sidewinder snake moves across the sand, each successive segment of its body is pushed down on the ground and then lifted off in turn—like the treads of a caterpillar tractor, or the segments of a wheel.

single central axis. Instead, it creates a succession of axes by continually curving its body from side to side as it moves forward.

Sidewinders are desert snakes, inhabiting dry regions of North America. Because they usually live on soft sand, they cannot move by wriggling their bodies as most snakes do. They must push downward against the sand to be sure of maintaining a firm grip. The advantage of the sidewinding motion is that it prevents the snake from sliding about on the shifting sands.

Sidewinders are seldom seen, although they may grow to a length of two feet or more. They spend their days partially buried in

sand, to escape the desert heat, and only at night do they move around. Many people who live in areas where sidewinders are common have never seen the snake, but have sometimes seen its distinctive parallel tracks.

Horned vipers and puff adders use a sidewinding motion to get across African deserts, and some other snakes will "sidewind" when placed on glass.

Because the sidewinder does not hold its tail in its mouth to form a real wheel, it doesn't have just one axis, but creates a succession of axes by continually curving its body from side to side as it moves forward. It leaves behind a series of parallel tracks that are at right angles to the direction in which it is traveling.

Spreading the Load

It is fun to go walking in the snow, but it is not always easy. Sometimes the snow is so deep that our every step is a major effort, and we don't seem to be getting anywhere. In countries where deep snow is common, people often prepare themselves for winter excursions by strapping on a pair of snowshoes. These large, flat shoes permit the wearer's weight to be distributed over a fairly wide area and keep him from sinking into snowbanks or deep drifts.

People who want snowshoes must either make them or buy them. Some animals are more fortunate. They grow their own snowshoes to carry them through the winter. One such animal, the snowshoe rabbit, got its name because of its large, fur-covered feet. Snowshoe rabbits and lynxes begin to grow new fur on their feet shortly before the beginning of winter. The new fur increases the size of their feet, giving them a larger surface area and preventing them from sinking as they walk. By the time the lynx has finished growing its winter shoes, its feet are entirely covered with fur. In summer, the lynx leaves the imprints of pads on the ground; but in winter, when the undersides of its feet are cloaked in fur, the lynx leaves large, round footprints in which no trace of a pad can be seen.

The snowshoe rabbit moves over the snow easily because of the hairy mats on the soles of its feet. Man has to strap on his mats in the form of snowshoes. Because these are so large, they distribute the weight over an area larger than the foot, and keep him from sinking into snowdrifts. Thus a man can even move fast enough to have a snowshoe race.

The lynx is another animal that moves easily over soft snow—thanks to its broad, furry feet.

Birds' feet are variously adapted for moving on different surfaces. The ptarmigan sprouts a fine pair of snowshoes, made of tufts of feathers. A similar growth helps the Asian sand grouse to move quickly over shifting sands. Where a man might travel in a vehicle with low-pressure tires that spread the weight to prevent sinking, a bird may move about on broad, thickly feathered toes or very long, slender toes. Herons, which spend much of their time walking on soft mud, have slender toes that are spaced widely apart Lily-trotters have longer toes that permit them to tread delicately on the surface of giant water lilies.

Some animals have solved the problem of moving on soft or shifting surfaces by developing long, stiltlike legs. Creatures that live on the oozy bottom of the sea must travel quickly and lightly so that they do not sink into the abyssal mud. Deep-sea crabs, for instance, have developed legs that are grotesquely long in comparison with their bodies. The sea spiders, which also live in the deep sea, are uniquely adapted for life in these perilous surroundings. Not only are their legs very long—sometimes three or four times the length of the body—but their bodies are also extremely light. Some sea spiders are so streamlined that their body has been reduced to almost nothing. There may not even be room inside the sea spider's body for all of its essential organs, so that some are located in the joints of its legs.

Left: The heron spends a great deal of time fishing in shallow waters, and needs its long, slender, widely spaced toes for moving about in the soft mud.

Below: Spreading its weight over eight legs, the sea spider hardly has any body at all. In fact, most of its organs, including the stomach, are in its legs. The sea spider moves easily over the ooze at the bottom of the sea.

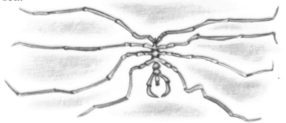

Water hyacinths float easily because their bulbous stalks are full of air. In principle they are not unlike the floating rafts used when astronauts "splash down" in the sea after returning from a space mission.

Paddles, Floats and Sails

If we wish to travel by water, we can choose among dozens of different types of vessels, from the Eskimo kayak to the ocean liner. Although man is the only creature to have designed and built boats to carry him across the surface of the water, many of the ideas he has explored for this purpose originated millions of years ago in the structure of various animals and plants. An obvious example is the rubber raft, which is simply a thin rubber skin filled with air. This is very much like the so-called "floating tissue" of some water plants. Floating tissue is quite loose, and contains large air spaces. A plant such as the water hyacinth floats easily because its bulbous stalks, which look thick and heavy, are actually composed mainly of air.

A large jellyfish called the Portuguese man-of-war also has a gas-filled float. This float not only acts as a raft; it also works as a sail. The man-of-war's sail is pale blue or greenish, and about six inches long. It looks roughly like half of a blown-up balloon sticking up out of the water. The sail is permanently set at a slight angle to the many long tentacles, hidden below the water's surface, which make up the rest of the jellyfish's body. A group of these jellyfish seen together always have their sails set at the same angle. This is probably because the wind blows them together, while those with their sails set at a different angle are carried off in another direction.

The Portuguese man-of-war, a jellyfish, floats and sails the seas. Its float is a bladder filled with gas and topped with a sail-like crest.

Paddles and oars are far more common in nature than either the raft or the sail. Many animals have flattened, blade-like limbs which they move rhythmically to propel themselves forward. A turtle, for example, has limbs that are shaped very much like canoe paddles. When a turtle swims, it first pushes against the water with the broad blade of the paddle. Then, as it moves forward, it "feathers" the paddle, holding it at an oblique angle to the direction of its course, to avoid exerting any pressure against the water. An experienced oarsman does the same thing, alternately pushing the blade of his oar broadside against the water, and feathering it as he raises it in the air.

One very skillful oarsman is a beetle called the water boatman. The water boatman has enlarged hind legs, set far back along the body, which function as an efficient pair of oars. These legs are blade-shaped, and are edged with a fringe of stiff hairs which increase the area available for pushing against the water. The beetle's body is oval and somewhat flattened, rather like a small but very seaworthy boat. Some water boatmen actually row themselves along upside-down in the water. These back-swimmers, as they are sometimes called, look even more like small boats than do other water boatmen. The water boatmen normally work their oars simultaneously, but they can also move one oar at a time, if they wish to turn about in small spaces.

When swimming, a turtle uses its limbs very much the way a good oarsman uses a canoe paddle. Similarly, the back-swimmer, a beetle, rows itself through the water.

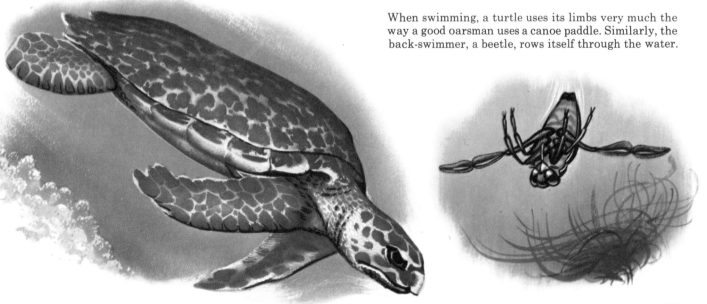

Aqualungs and Snorkels

An air-breathing animal cannot breathe underwater. Therefore, if it is going to stay underwater for any length of time, it must carry with it a supply of air. A human diver who intends to remain submerged for more than a minute or so will equip himself according to the kind of dive he is making. For long, deep dives, he will wear a diving suit and helmet, connected by a long hose to a supply of air at the surface. For shorter and shallower dives, he will use an aqualung, which allows him more freedom to swim. This consists of one or more tanks of air strapped to the diver's back, plus a short hose leading to a mouthpiece through which he inhales as much air as he needs. For dives in shallow water, the diver may use a device called a snorkel. This is a short breathing tube with a mouthpiece. The free end of the tube sticks up above the water, and allows the diver to swim, face downward, near the surface, and receive a constant supply of air.

Other air-breathing creatures which make the water their habitat have natural diving equipment. A large insect, the whirligig beetle (or the great water beetle), can supply itself with enough air to stay underwater for an average of eight-and-a-half minutes at a time. When this beetle needs to breathe, it rises to the surface and pushes its tail end through the surface of the water. At the very end of the beetle's body are two breathing tubes. When the beetle pushes

Just as a diver uses an aqualung to hold his supply of air underwater, the whirligig beetle carries a bubble of air attached to its tail when diving. It can also carry an air supply under its wing-cases. Usually, however, it skims about on the surface of the water.

through the surface, bringing these tubes into contact with the outside air, it depresses the end of its abdomen, creating a space directly under its wing-cases. The beetle fills this space with a bubble of air, and then raises its abdomen, so that it is carrying on its back a sealed air chamber, like an aqualung tank, stocked with a reserve supply of air.

The silver water beetle collects and stores air in a different way. This beetle has a silvery appearance because it is covered with hundreds of tiny air bubbles. The breathing tubes of the silver water beetle are located along its sides. When it rises to the surface for air, it comes up headfirst, and uses its antennae to scoop in air along both sides of its body.

Two kinds of pond-dwelling insects are equipped with a snorkel-type breathing apparatus. These are the water scorpion and the stick scorpion (or water stick insect), both of which have a long, slender breathing tube at the end of the abdomen. When they need to take in a fresh air supply, they rise to the surface of the water, often climbing up the stem of a water plant, and push the end of their breathing tube through the surface. They remain quietly breathing for several moments before submerging again.

Water stick insects (above, far right) and water scorpions (right) are members of the same family. Both live underwater and have breathing siphons which take in air from the surface—rather like a diver's snorkel.

Below: The silver water beetle at top left spends more time underwater than the whirligig beetle, but it, too, must breathe air. It comes to the surface to collect its supply, then goes underwater again, carrying a bubble of air between its body and wing-cases and a film of air on its underside.

A water spider constructs its diving bell by spinning a silk web that is fine enough to hold air. Then it travels back and forth between the bell and the surface of the water, bringing a new bubble of air each time until the bell is filled with air.

Franz Kessler's diving bell of 1616 was like a drinking glass turned upside-down. Enough air was trapped inside the bell to allow the diver to put his head in and breathe between dives. Edward Halley's diving bell of 1720 (right) was a more sophisticated version, allowing the air supply in the bell to be replenished. Both the diving bell and the extra air supply—in a separate lead cask—were lowered from a ship.

Diving Bell

The water spider is an unusual spider, because, unlike all its relations, it lives permanently underwater. It does this even though it must breathe air to survive. In this sense, the spider is living in alien territory—it lives in the water, but it cannot breathe there. It solves this problem by building a diving bell, and filling it with bubbles of air which it brings from the surface.

Water spiders are common inhabitants of ponds and lakes in the temperate regions of Europe and Asia. If you live in one of these areas, you may be able to capture a water spider and watch it constructing its diving bell at home in a glass aquarium. The water spider is dark brown, with a darker, velvety abdomen. When it is swimming about, however, it looks like a piece of shining silver because of the glistening air bubbles that cling to its body. The spider begins building its diving bell by weaving a silken sheet, which is anchored at the corners to the stems or leaves of water plants. This sheet is made of the same sort of silk which land-dwelling

spiders use to build their webs. Like the land spiders, the water spider manufactures its own silk and releases it through openings in its body called spinnerets. The water spider's silken sheet is much more closely woven than an ordinary spider web, however. This close weaving is important, because the sheet forms a waterproof covering.

During the initial building operations, the spider survives on a single bubble of air, which can last for several hours. Once the water spider has completed the silken dome of its diving bell, it swims to the surface to collect a large air supply. It splashes about near the surface, swimming upside-down and kicking with its legs to make bubbles. Then the spider grasps a large air bubble between its hind legs and swims back to the dome it has built. The bubble is released inside the dome, and the spider returns to the surface for more air. It makes about eight to ten of these collecting trips in succession, and as the air supply inside the dome increases, the bell shape becomes more pro-

nounced. At last the dome resembles a squat silver thimble, and the water spider can turn its attention from collecting air to hunting for food. During the day, it waits inside the diving bell, with its front legs dangling down into the water, ready to pounce upon any water insect which swims within reach. At night, it ventures out in search of insects and small crustaceans, carrying a small bubble of air close to its breathing tubes.

Unlike the water spider, men do not live permanently inside diving bells. Diving bells have been used for about two thousand years as an aid in hunting for sunken treasures and carrying out underwater building operations. The earliest diving bells were actually bell-shaped chambers. Alexander the Great used such a chamber in the fourth century B.C., when he attempted to recover the contents of a sunken treasure ship. During the past century, round enclosed chambers such as the bathysphere have been developed, in which men have been able to travel downward and explore the deep, dark canyons of the sea.

Below: Jacques Cousteau's *Conshelf III* was a chamber that housed six aquanauts for three weeks of Mediterranean undersea research in 1965. Inside the sphere was a kitchen, dining room, shower, lavatory and bunkroom—besides all the data-gathering equipment. The outside chassis held a mesh pantry box, ballast tanks, and a container that stored nine tons of fresh water.

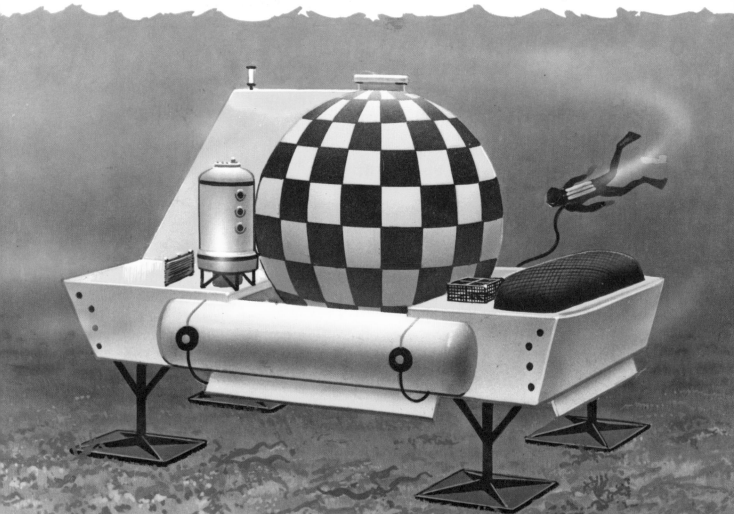

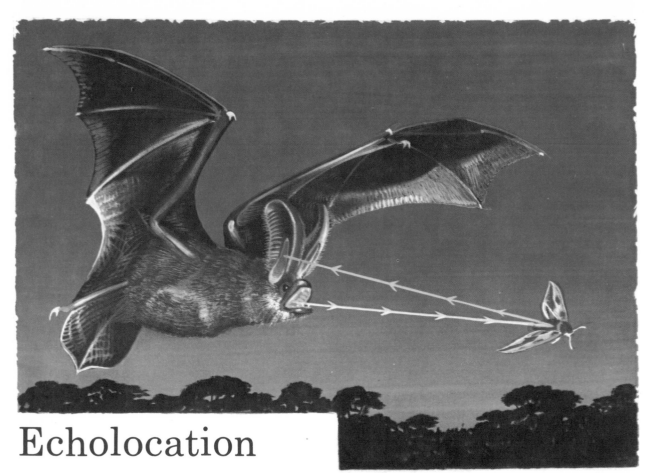

Echolocation

Bats are nocturnal creatures. They hunt by night, and often fly in pitch-darkness. Yet they are not hampered by lack of light, for bats have an amazing ability to "see" with their ears. A bat explores its surroundings by issuing high-pitched screams, and listening for their echoes. The pulses of sound emitted by the bat are reflected back from any object in its path. The bat hears these reflected sounds, or echoes, and its brain then interprets them to form an auditory "picture" of what lies ahead. This system of locating objects by means of echoes is called echolocation.

Bat cries are too high-pitched for humans to hear. They fall into the high-frequency range known as ultrasound. The bat cries in this high voice to produce a sharper echo than is possible with lower-frequency sounds. When the bat is stationary, it cries about eight times per second. The moment it takes off, however, its cries increase, reaching perhaps 200 bursts a second as it approaches close to an obstacle. Thus it receives a constant stream of information as it nears its goal, and

Bats use hearing the same way humans use sight. Man gets information about his surroundings by receiving and analyzing reflected light rays, and the bat "sees" its environment by means of reflected sound waves, or echoes. The bat emits high-pitched cries at a rate of 8 to 200 per second, so it is constantly receiving echoes.

All bats have big ears, but the ears of the long-eared bat are even longer than its body. The external ear, or pinna, is the receiver. The spear-shaped cartilege, called the tragus, probably picks up echoes coming from the side.

EMISSION	(head)	85–1,100 cycles per second
	(bat)	10,000–120,000 c.p.s.
RECEPTION	(head)	20–20,000 c.p.s.
	(bat)	1,000–120,000 c.p.s.

This chart shows the frequency range emitted and received by a man and a bat. Frequency refers to the number of cycles, or complete vibrations, per second, and is related to pitch.

Radar is used to "see" through a fog at sea. Radio waves are sent out by transmitters; their echoes are received by sensitive antennae and interpreted on a radar screen.

by rapidly analyzing the numerous echoes it receives, it can "see" even tiny insects.

Bats and dolphins (next page) are the most well-known "echolocaters," but it is thought that other animals may also use this system. The oil bird of South America is known to navigate dark jungle caves by making a clicking noise and listening for the echoes.

Men cannot distinguish fast-returning echoes as well as bats can. Nevertheless, sailors have long used a primitive form of echolocation to locate obstructions in fog or darkness. The technique is to produce a sharp shout or whistle, and then to listen for echoes from rocks or other objects believed to be in the immediate vicinity.

The system of echolocation most often compared with that of bats is radar (Radio Aircraft Detection and Ranging). Many people say that bats have "radar." But radar systems do not use sound pulses to locate objects; instead, they employ electromagnetic waves, called radio waves. These radio waves are used for location purposes

the same way as sound waves are. The radio waves are sent out by radio transmitters, and their echoes are received by sensitive antennae and interpreted by electronic apparatus. Electronic radar can pick up objects at far greater distances than can "bat radar." However, considering the differences in their equipment, the bat's echolocation system is almost as efficient as man's.

Radar was first developed for the detection of distant aircraft, and was vitally important in the location of enemy airplanes during World War II. It has since been put to various uses, including air traffic control, the detection of speeding automobiles, the tracking of storms, and the investigation of the surfaces of other planets. Meteorologists can gain useful information about tomorrow's weather by listening to echoes from raindrops, ice crystals, and so on. Radar also helps in weather control. A radar operator on the ground can study the clouds and inform pilots in the air how best to carry out cloud-seeding operations aimed at producing rain.

Dolphins can locate their prey by sending out sound waves, listening for their echoes, and then analyzing them. Similarly, a dolphin that has been trained to catch a ring dropped in the water can do the trick blindfolded because he locates the ring by echolocation.

One of the friendliest and most intelligent of all animals is the dolphin. Dolphins are sea-dwelling mammals, averaging about eight feet in length. They are warm-blooded, air-breathing creatures, and therefore must come to the surface about every seven to ten minutes to exhale and to take in a fresh supply of air. The dolphin is a very fast swimmer, moving at an average speed of ten nautical miles an hour. Often it must swim through dim or muddy waters where visibility is so poor that it can see for only a few inches ahead. To maintain its speed with safety, the dolphin must be able to locate and identify objects at distances many yards ahead. What it sees during its trips to the surface cannot provide an accurate picture of what lies under the water. Dolphins overcome this problem by using a system of echolocation, rather like the bats', to investigate their surroundings. This system involves sending out sound signals through the water, listening for their echoes, and then analyzing these echoes to form a sound picture of the environment. In this way they can "see" or sense the sea bottom, the hulls of ships, food fish, other dolphins, and so on. Dolphins make use of the same navigational tactic when swimming through the water as bats do when they fly through the air on a dark night. Like bats, dolphins employ high-frequency sounds, or ultrasounds, in order to gain a sonic image.

A swimming dolphin emits sound waves of varying lengths. Longer wavelengths enable it to judge the location of the ocean floor and of any large objects within a range of a few hundred yards. Shorter wavelengths are emitted when it wishes to "see" something in finer detail. The dolphin beams its sound

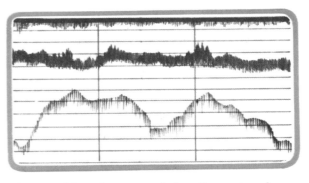

Man uses his underwater echolocation system, known as sonar, in the same way as the dolphin: he can analyze the outline of the sea floor, as shown on the screen above.

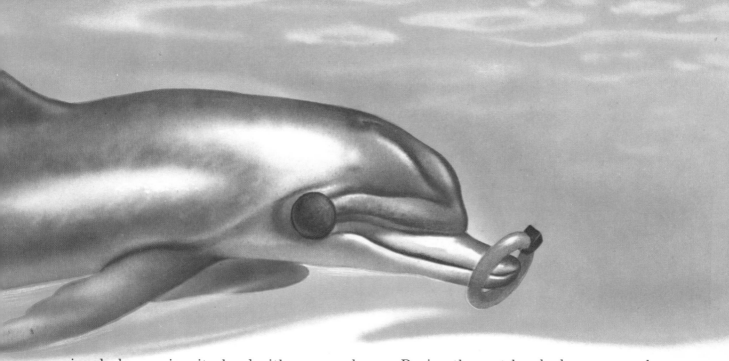

signals by moving its head either up and down or back and forth, much as we might move a flashlight in order to beam the light over the contents of a dark room.

Some of the sounds transmitted by the dolphin are absorbed by the objects they strike; others are reflected to form echoes. Dolphins can judge differences in materials according to the echoes they receive. For example, the echoes reflected by wood sound different to the dolphin than those reflected by metal or by the body of another dolphin. Thus the animal learns not only the size but also the nature of any objects surrounding it.

During the past hundred years, men have developed a system of echolocation for use underwater. Known as sonar, this system employs sound waves as signals to locate objects at distances of up to 2,500 yards and more. Sonar was invented during World War I, to help detect submarines. Most of the underwater listening during that war consisted simply of monitoring accidental sounds made by propeller-driven ships. The deliberate transmission of signals for echo sounding was not much used. By World War II, however, sonar had been developed to a high degree of efficiency as a means of submarine detection.

Before sonar was perfected, ships were often fitted only with receivers. Underwater bells connected to light-houses emitted vibrations which warned ships of navigational hazards in any weather.

Parachutes

Anyone who has a garden is apt to complain that weeds are "spreading" through the grass and flowerbeds. We may wonder how a plant, which is stationary and rooted to the ground, can spread itself in this way, sometimes appearing suddenly in an area where it has never grown before. The answer lies in the various ways in which the seeds of plants are dispersed. Several seeds have mechanisms which use the power of the wind to carry them over long distances. Some wind-borne seeds are very small and light, and are balanced in a way that allows them to float for long periods in the air. Others have wing-shaped appendages, which enable them to drift along with the air currents.

Perhaps the most efficient of all wind-dispersal devices is a sort of natural parachute, composed of tufts of fine hairs. These soft, plumelike tufts radiate outward from an individual seed, or from a small fruit containing a number of seeds. When the parachute is floating through the air, the featherweight plumes support the fruit or seed, so that it does not fall rapidly to the ground, but instead is buoyed up on the breeze. Among the many plants which have such parachute devices are the willow herb, the valerian, the milkweed, the goatsbeard, the clematis, and the poplar and willow trees. The most efficient design of all is that of the dandelion, which, as a result, is one of the commonest of all weeds. Everyone who has

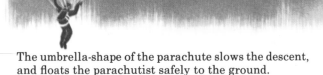

The umbrella-shape of the parachute slows the descent, and floats the parachutist safely to the ground.

Several plants use parachutes to scatter their seeds. The most efficient of these is the dandelion (right).

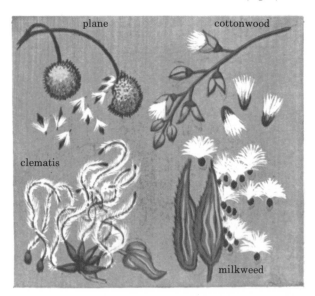

plane cottonwood clematis milkweed

seen these golden-yellow flowers growing wild will also be familiar with the soft, gray-white heads of the ripened flowers. These are sometimes called "dandelion clocks," and many children "tell time" by the number of breaths needed to blow the entire feathery mass into the wind.

According to legend, the first men to use a

parachute-like device were Chinese acrobats of the sixteenth century. These men attached umbrellas to their belts, and daringly jumped from the top of a high cliff, trusting that their descent would be gradual enough to keep them from being hurt. Modern parachutes are still designed with the basic umbrella-shaped canopy, but various improvements have been made over the centuries. By 1783, Sebastian le Normand, a French professor of physics and chemistry, had replaced the ribs and handle of the umbrella with cords running from the outer edge of the canopy. Later, parachutists discovered that steering could be improved by making holes in the canopy. This allowed some of the air to escape upward,

and prevented the parachute from being rocked about by air trying to escape under the sides.

In the seed parachute this problem is similarly prevented, since the "umbrella" is composed of separate tufts, and air travels freely through it.

Man-made parachutes have a variety of military and civilian uses. They are carried on commercial airplanes as safety devices, and are also used for cargo-dropping, airborne fire-fighting, and braking the speed of aircraft coming in for a landing. On the military front, paratroopers can be dropped into enemy territory which vehicles and infantrymen could not penetrate.

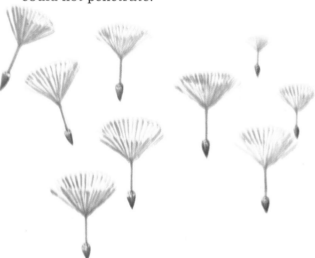

Leonardo da Vinci designed a parachute in the fifteenth century, and wrote: "If a man have a tent made of linen of which the apertures have all been stopped up . . . he will be able to throw himself down from any great height without sustaining any injury." The first men actually to use a parachute-like device were probably Chinese acrobats, who attached umbrellas to their belts and jumped off high cliffs.

The command module of an Apollo spacecraft splashes down. When the module gets down to 24,000 feet, parachutes blossom out to slow the final descent.

Powered Flight

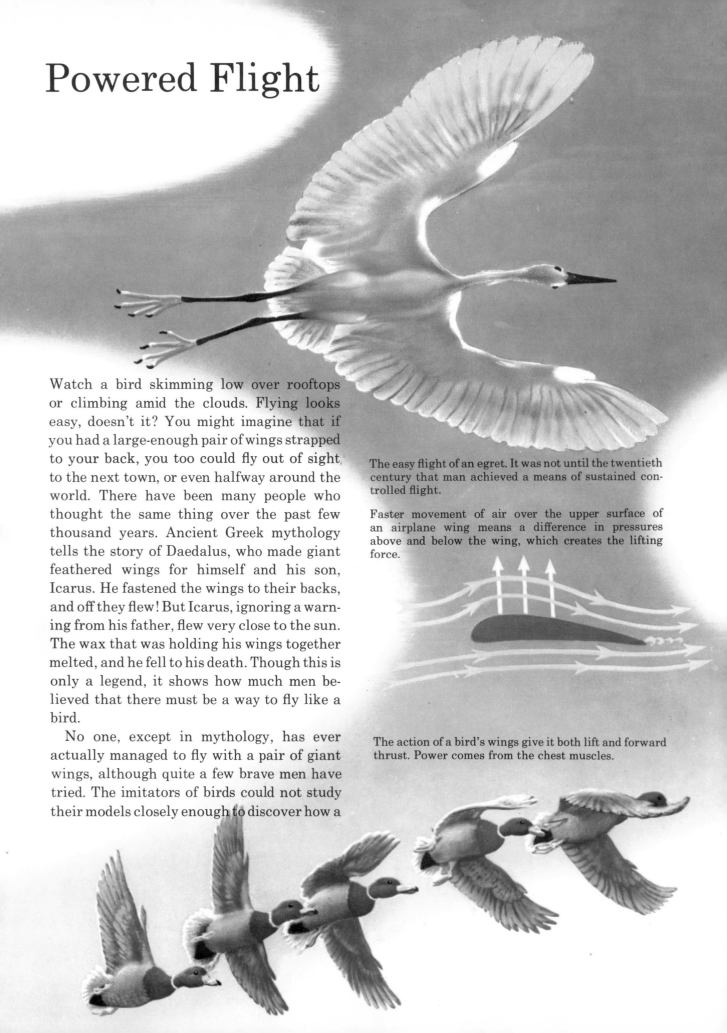

Watch a bird skimming low over rooftops or climbing amid the clouds. Flying looks easy, doesn't it? You might imagine that if you had a large-enough pair of wings strapped to your back, you too could fly out of sight, to the next town, or even halfway around the world. There have been many people who thought the same thing over the past few thousand years. Ancient Greek mythology tells the story of Daedalus, who made giant feathered wings for himself and his son, Icarus. He fastened the wings to their backs, and off they flew! But Icarus, ignoring a warning from his father, flew very close to the sun. The wax that was holding his wings together melted, and he fell to his death. Though this is only a legend, it shows how much men believed that there must be a way to fly like a bird.

No one, except in mythology, has ever actually managed to fly with a pair of giant wings, although quite a few brave men have tried. The imitators of birds could not study their models closely enough to discover how a

The easy flight of an egret. It was not until the twentieth century that man achieved a means of sustained controlled flight.

Faster movement of air over the upper surface of an airplane wing means a difference in pressures above and below the wing, which creates the lifting force.

The action of a bird's wings give it both lift and forward thrust. Power comes from the chest muscles.

bird really flies. Only high-speed photography gives us a clear picture of a bird's movements. The airplane was developed as a purely mechanical flying machine; it was not copied from nature. Only after the machine was invented were physicists able to apply their knowledge of flight mechanics to the study of the flight of birds. They saw that a bird's wings perform a double role. Not only do they provide an upward lift, like the wings of an airplane, but they also propel the bird forward, just as the airplane's propeller pushes it through the air. (The power behind the propeller comes from the engine, just as the bird's power comes from its strong chest muscles.)

the pressure above it. This creates a lifting force and results in the wings' being lifted up and, at the same time, dragged slightly backward. In aircraft with propellers, the propeller compensates for this backward drag. By thrusting against the air, the engine-driven propeller induces a forward motion in the aircraft.

The inner part of the bird's wing corresponds to the wing of an airplane, providing an upward lift during flight. The outer part of the bird's wing serves the same function as an airplane propeller—it moves the bird forward through the air. The bird's wing tips (the outer parts of the wings) move in a semicircle as the bird flies, pushing

The wings of both birds and airplanes are held at an angle to the direction of the air flowing past them. Because of this angle, air flows faster over the upper surface of the wing than it does over the lower surface. The air pressure below the wing is greater than

firmly against the air. The greatest forward motion is produced on the upstroke, when the bird raises its wings and moves the wing tips upward and backward. This pressure of the wing tips against the air propels the bird forward.

The albatross is a heavy bird with vast wings but small chest muscles. Having very little power, it therefore relies on a sustained wind for flight. Similarly, a glider, having no engine, is also dependent on the wind and the skill of the pilot.

Gliding Flight

It is possible to fly through the air, reaching heights of 40,000 feet and more, in a plane that has no engine at all. Such an aircraft is called a glider or sailplane. The pilot of a glider depends entirely upon gravity and air currents when he flies. The wings of the aircraft are stationary—they cannot flap, and there is no internal source of power to propel the glider forward. Still, the pilot can rise and soar into the clouds, circle upward like an eagle, and glide downwind like a giant sea bird.

Gliders are launched into the air by means of a cable fastened to a windlass in a moving car or an engine-powered aircraft. The light glider is raised to a height of about 1,000 feet from the ground before it is released from the launching apparatus. Then the pilot is on his own, and must use his experience and skill to stay aloft, fly where he wants to go, and land safely.

Gliders usually travel downward along a sloping course. The angle this course makes in relation to the ground determines how quickly the glider will lose height. Just as a sled will travel faster down a steep hill than a gradual slope, so a glider will descend faster when flying at a steep angle to the ground. Therefore, the best gliding angle is a very flat one, allowing the lifting force which the air exerts against the wings to compensate for the downward accelerating force of gravity.

A glider does not always travel downward, however. If it did, it could not remain in the air for long. Strong upward currents of air can carry the glider high into the sky. Riding these upward currents is known as soaring. Soaring is most often done by circling

The *Draco*, or flying dragon, can glide for fifty feet. Folds of membrane are stretched on several pairs of ribs to form the "wings."

The flying fish gets airborne by swimming very fast and spreading its long fins. It glides for about ten seconds before diving or splashing down on its belly.

Below: The flying phalanger of Australia. Folds of skin between the limbs are outstretched in a gliding leap that may transport the animal 100 yards.

within patches of rising air called thermals. A thermal consists of warm air that has expanded and grown lighter than the air surrounding it. Because of this, it rises, and the skillful pilot can maneuver his glider to soar up along with it.

Most people who go gliding regard it merely as an exciting sport, although a few are involved in experimental flights to aid meteorologists and aircraft designers. For birds, and even for some mammals, reptiles and fish, gliding is a useful way of traveling. The group of reptiles which glide are called *Draco*, or flying dragons. They are small lizards, with brilliant coloring; by stretching their scaly "wings," which are really flaps of skin, they can glide more than fifty feet from one tree to another.

Flying squirrels also glide among the trees, launching themselves from a high branch, and coming to rest on a lower one. Their "wings" are furry membranes, which they learn to use at the age of three months.

Birds—nature's experts on flight—are, of course, the best gliders. Broad-winged birds, such as eagles and vultures, are expert riders of thermal currents. Using these and other upward currents, the great birds soar constantly upward without moving their wings. The best of all gliders is the narrow-winged albatross. This sea bird, whose wings span eleven feet or more, can glide for hours above the surface of the sea, rising and falling with an easy, spiraling motion.

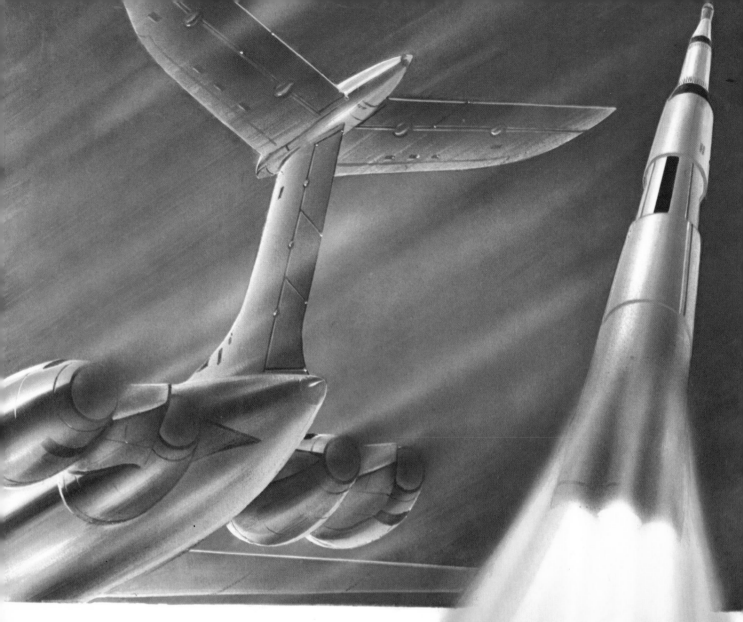

Jet Propulsion

The forward motion of a jet plane is produced by jets of exhaust gases, which escape at great speed through nozzles at the rear of the plane. Jet propulsion is also the lifting and driving force for rockets.

One of the fastest ways of traveling around the world today is in a jet airplane. Jets have been developed only within the past thirty years, but the pace of this development has been truly phenomenal. The modern "jumbo jet," which can carry more than 500 people, can fly at speeds of nearly 700 miles an hour, and this is by no means the fastest aircraft speed. The engine of a jet aircraft provides the necessary power for travel by "jet propulsion." Air is taken in at the front of the aircraft, and passes first into a compressor and then into a combustion chamber, where it is mixed with fuel and burned. The results

of this burning are exhaust gases. These gases escape at great speed through nozzles at the rear of the airplane. When the gases are ejected, they produce a forward thrust which propels the jet through the air. This is how jet propulsion works in an aircraft: the forward motion is produced by the ejection of jets of exhaust gases.

Jet propulsion works according to a principle set out by the mathematician Sir Isaac Newton: "To every action there is an equal and opposite reaction." In the case of the jet aircraft, we see this principle in operation; for the plane moves forward with the exact

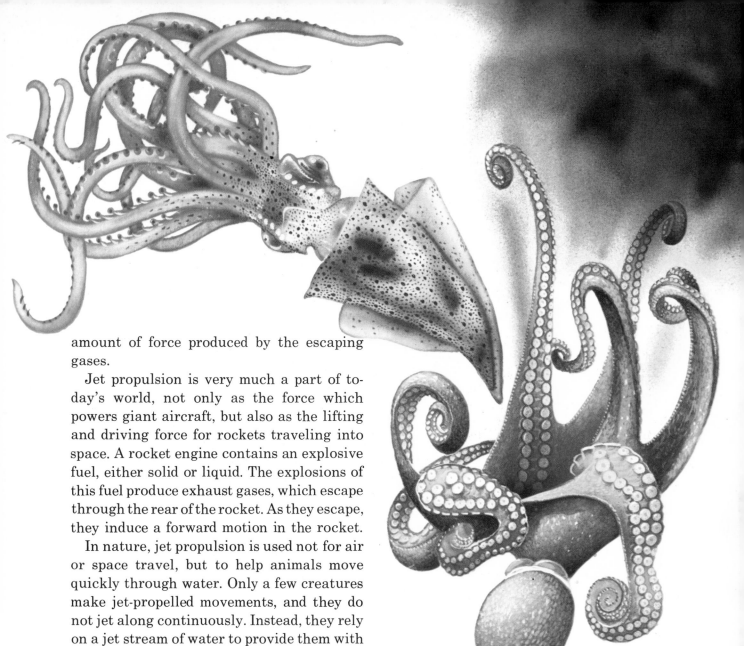

amount of force produced by the escaping gases.

Jet propulsion is very much a part of today's world, not only as the force which powers giant aircraft, but also as the lifting and driving force for rockets traveling into space. A rocket engine contains an explosive fuel, either solid or liquid. The explosions of this fuel produce exhaust gases, which escape through the rear of the rocket. As they escape, they induce a forward motion in the rocket.

In nature, jet propulsion is used not for air or space travel, but to help animals move quickly through water. Only a few creatures make jet-propelled movements, and they do not jet along continuously. Instead, they rely on a jet stream of water to provide them with a sudden burst of speed. A well-known jet-propelled creature is the squid, which looks like a slender rocket with a mass of waving tentacles at one end. Squid are found in waters all over the world. Some are giant creatures, growing up to fifty feet in length, with a body perhaps fifteen feet long and the rest taken up by the huge tentacles. The kind of squid that fishermen use for bait have an overall length of about ten inches. The squid's body is surrounded by a muscular sac called the mantle. The sac extends as far as the creature's head, and is open at the head end. As the squid swims, water enters the mantle. The muscles of the mantle then contract, forcing the water out through a tubelike structure called the siphon,

The squid (above, left) and octopus (above) can use jet propulsion for sudden bursts of speed. They can also eject ink in their jet streams to confuse predators.

which extends beyond the mantle's open edge. A stream of water is released that propels the squid quite rapidly in the direction opposite to that of the jet's flow. The siphon can be pointed either forward or backward, enabling the squid to use its jet stream to move quickly toward prey or away from enemies.

Both the squid and the octopus, which can also travel by jet propulsion, use their jet streams to confuse their enemies, by forcing an inky liquid out through the siphon.

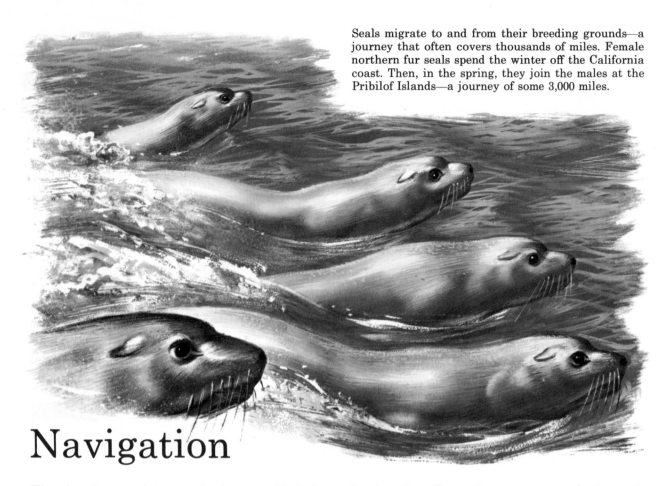

Seals migrate to and from their breeding grounds—a journey that often covers thousands of miles. Female northern fur seals spend the winter off the California coast. Then, in the spring, they join the males at the Pribilof Islands—a journey of some 3,000 miles.

Navigation

The Arctic tern is a sun-loving sea bird. It nests in the Arctic during the northern summer (June to August); then, as soon as summer is over, the tern flies south to spend another summer in Antarctic regions. Twice yearly it migrates from pole to pole, crossing continents and oceans. Using neither compass nor map, it can fly up to 11,000 miles each way without getting lost.

Arctic terns are among the thousands of different creatures that migrate long distances in search of warmth or suitable breeding grounds. Fish, turtles, butterflies, countless flocks of birds, and many other animals perform amazing feats of navigation when they travel. Green turtles swim more than 1,200 miles out from the Brazilian mainland to reach nesting sites on tiny Ascension Island. This remote island in the Atlantic is so difficult to locate that human navigators using complex instruments sometimes fail to find it.

If you have a good memory, you can travel for quite a distance relying on familiar landmarks. But when you travel through unfamiliar country or across vast empty stretches of ocean, landmarks are of no avail. Men have learned to make maps, and to find their bearings according to the position of certain heavenly bodies in the sky. Celestial navigation involves the finding and measuring of the positions of the sun, moon, stars, and planets. Navigators use instruments to discover the angle that a certain celestial body makes with the horizon. Then they make calculations based on tables to determine the point on Earth directly below the celestial body at that particular time. Further observations allow the navigator to calculate the relationship between that point and his immediate location.

Animals navigate without benefit of charts, tables, or instruments, but many do rely on clues in the sky to guide them. Bees, wasps, and other insects are guided by the sun during their daily flights. Migrating birds depend so completely upon the heavenly bodies for direction-finding that they are

The Arctic tern travels up to 11,000 miles, from the Arctic to the Antarctic, every year. It nests in the north from June to August, then flies south to spend another summer at the bottom of the world. Each journey takes about three months.

Migrating birds depend almost completely on the position of the sun and the stars. To test this instinct, Dr. Sauer placed young warblers, raised in confinement, inside a special planetarium. The "sky" in the planetarium was lit by artificial stars, arranged to look like major constellations. The warblers instinctively began flying in the direction normally taken by migratory night flights. When the sky was rotated through 90 degrees, the birds altered their course accordingly.

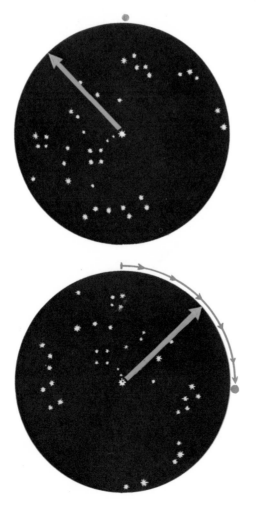

often grounded if a heavy bank of clouds obscures the sky. If the clouds are low, the birds will fly above them to keep the sun or stars in sight. When the clouds are too dense for this, however, the flock pauses for rest and food until the sky is clear again.

Zoologists have conducted numerous experiments to prove that birds navigate by the sun and stars. One such experiment was conceived by a German scientist, Dr. E. G. F. Sauer. Young warblers that had been raised in confinement were placed inside a specially built planetarium. The planetarium "sky" was lit by artificial stars, arranged to look like the major constellations. The warblers, which migrate by night, instinctively began to fly in the direction normally taken by migratory flights. When Dr. Sauer rotated the sky through 90 degrees, the birds altered their course accordingly.

Like Dr. Sauer's warblers, all migrating animals follow their instincts. They are not seeking a goal so much as following an impulse to keep moving along a particular route. They may navigate by the sun and stars, by landmarks, or by odors. Some zoologists believe that animals can also navigate by responding to sensations produced by the earth's magnetic field. Whichever way a migrating animal navigates, there is apparently some instinctive "pre-programming" that tells it which way to travel and where to stop.

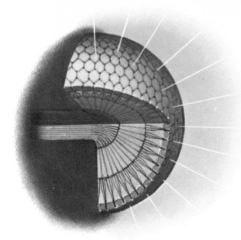

The compound eye of the horsefly is made up of thousands of tiny simple eyes, or facets. Each facet is connected to its own nerve ending, and thereby sends its own tiny picture to the brain. The resulting image is a mosaic of all the impressions from all the facets.

The water flea faces the sun so that the light is striking its compound eye; then it simply follows the sun.

Sun Compasses

An insect's eye is a very complicated organ. Known as a compound eye, it is made up of many separate, simpler "eyes." Each of these separate eyes, or facets, contains a tiny lens and a group of retinal cells; and each is connected to a network of nerve cells that send signals to the brain. This means that every individual facet is a mechanism for seeing. An insect such as a dragonfly has thousands of facets in each of its two large compound eyes. Every facet registers a small section of the scene confronting the dragonfly. Thus, what the insect sees is a total picture composed of thousands of tiny individual impressions.

It is amazing to think of a structure as complex as the compound eye being part of an insect. But insects are a lot more complicated than they look. The compound eyes of certain insects, for instance, have more than one function. These insects do not merely use their two large eyes to see; they also use them as part of an elaborate navigational system. A great many creatures (in-

cluding man) navigate according to the position of the sun in the sky. In a simple way, so does an animal such as the water flea, this navigation being merely a matter of heading constantly in the sun's direction. The water flea places itself so that the sun's light always shines from straight ahead, directly into its compound eyes. This type of navigation allows the water flea very little freedom of movement; it is virtually a slave of the sunlight, moving always as the sun moves. For an animal to plot a more complicated course by the sun, it must be able to compensate for the movements of the sun across the sky. Its sensory equipment must register the fact that the sun's position is altering, and also judge how far the sun has moved during a period of time.

The ability to navigate by the sun is known as a sun-compass sense. Among insects, this sense is present in a primitive form in water fleas, dung beetles and others, and in a far more sophisticated form among bees, wasps, hornets, ants, and some other species. An

Navigation by the sun is more sophisticated in bees than in water fleas. Bees are constantly making allowances for the sun's change of position—as well as their own. Thus, when flying a straight course, they expect the sun to strike first one lens, then the adjoining one, and so on. Moths use the light of the sun or the moon to guide their flight. If this light is always striking the eye at a certain angle, the moth is assured of a straight course. But trouble starts when the moth mistakes a local light source for the more distant one. If it attempts to fly so that *this* light is always hitting its eye at the same angle, it will go into a spiral, become totally confused, and begin again. This explains the moth's "fascination" with light.

insect such as a bee can alter its course continually, making corrections as the sun moves across the sky. It can do this because of the way in which its compound eyes, its brain, and a very accurate internal "clock" work together. This clock is not a piece of equipment located somewhere inside the insect; it is a regular biological rhythm which governs all aspects of its life. This rhythm tells the creature the time of day, as well as the season of the year. This is necessary for the insect to understand the sun's movements—to know, for example, whether the sun is rising or setting.

If we can understand how a bee manages to fly on a straight course, we will gain some idea of how the sun compass works. As the bee flies, direct sunlight strikes the lens of a single facet in one of its compound eyes. If it continues flying for ten minutes, direct sunlight will no longer fall on that lens, but on an adjoining one. Now, if the bee were unaware that time had passed, and that the sun had moved, it might alter its straight course to keep the sunlight falling on the original lens. But the bee's internal clock, and its inborn knowledge of where the sun is at a given time, tell it that it should continue flying directly onward without changing its direction.

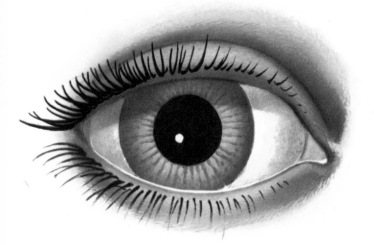

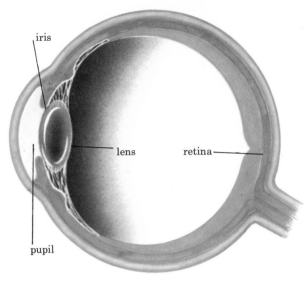

The Camera Eye

There are many different types of eyes in the animal kingdom. Some are simple "eye-spots," registering only light and darkness, while others are extremely complex, permitting accurate, three-dimensional color vision. Men have invented a number of devices that are similar in principle to various kinds of animal eyes, but even more striking is the comparison between the camera and the human eye.

The human eye is perhaps the most highly developed of all animal eyes, and is often referred to by biologists as a "camera eye." Light enters the eye through an opening called the pupil. This is the solid, black center of the eye, and is surrounded by a ring

The similarities between the camera and the human eye are striking. The eye admits light through a pupil; the camera admits light through the aperture. The size of the pupil, and therefore the amount of light let into the eye, is controlled by the muscles of the iris; just as the iris diaphragm controls the size of the aperture and the amount of light let into the camera. The lens in the eye is the most important element in bending the light rays and focusing the image; in the camera, also, the lens is the device that focuses the rays to achieve a sharp image. The image that falls on the retina of the eye is a clear, upside-down picture of what the eye is seeing—like the upside-down image on the camera film.

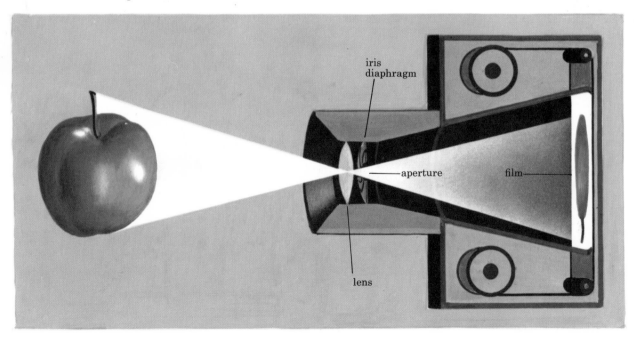

of muscle fibers called the iris. It is the iris which gives the eye its particular color—blue, brown, green or gray. The function of the iris is to increase or decrease the size of the pupil, thus regulating the amount of light that passes into the eye.

When light enters the eye, it is traveling in straight lines. Structures behind the pupil bend the rays of light and focus them to a point. This bending is necessary to keep the light from spreading out and causing a fuzzy image. The first focusing structure in the eye is a transparent layer called the cornea. This bends the rays of light sharply inward toward each other. After passing through the cornea, the light travels through a colorless fluid, the aqueous humor, until it reaches the lens. The lens is the most important focusing device in the eye, and is made up of some 2,200 layers, each one of which bends the light very slightly inward. The lens completes the job of focusing, and the light travels onward, through a jellylike substance called the vitreous humor, to form an image on the back wall of the eye. The image that the light forms on this back wall, or retina, of the eye is a clear, upside-down picture of what the eye is seeing. A network of nerves conveys this inverted image to the brain, which "corrects" it, so that things appear to us rightside-up.

The camera is not as sophisticated or flexible an instrument as the human eye, but there are strong similarities between the two. The camera admits light through an opening called the aperture. The size of this aperture is controlled by a device called the iris diaphragm. Like the iris in the human eye, the iris diaphragm regulates the amount of light entering the camera. After the light has entered through the aperture, it passes through a lens, which focuses the rays to achieve a sharp image. This image is recorded on a piece of light-sensitive film. Like the image that falls on the retina of the eye, this camera image is upside-down. When the photographer removes the film from the camera, he can turn the picture whichever way he wants.

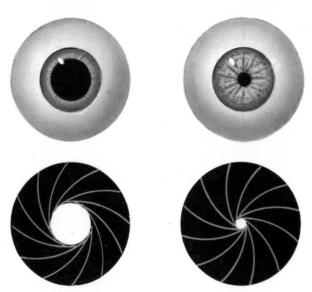

The pupil of the eye (top) and the aperture of the camera. The pupil, controlled by the iris, automatically grows large in dim light and small in bright light—thus always letting in the right amount of light. The iris diaphragm of the camera is also adjusted to bring the correct amount of light into the aperture.

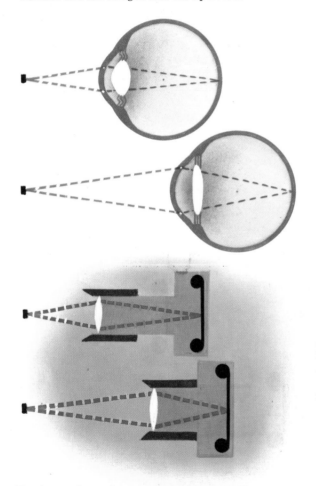

To change focus from a near object to a distant one or vice versa, the camera lens must be moved; for a distant shot the lens is nearer to the film than it is for a close-up. The human lens is more sophisticated; it stays in the same place, but changes shape, adjusting to the angle of the light rays in order to bend them.

57

Using Infrared Rays

If you were unable to see, hear or smell, your life would be very restricted. You could only sense objects and living creatures by touching them or by feeling the vibrations produced by their movements. Certainly you would have little hope of finding food for yourself. Not all creatures, however, would be as helpless as a human in such a situation.

The rattlesnake, and other members of the family of pit vipers to which it belongs, have proven themselves to be skillful hunters, even when deprived experimentally of the senses of smell, sight and hearing. These snakes have an extra sense, useful to them in night hunting. They are able to perceive the heat radiating from any warm body located within striking distance. This radiant heat, known as infrared radiation, is given off by all warm objects, both living and nonliving. The rattlesnake has two deep pits, located on either side of its head, which

"Heat-ray eyes" on either side of the rattlesnake's head are sensitive to infrared radiation. With them the snake can "see" any warm creature. With tapes on its eyes (below), it strikes with accuracy at a light bulb that is the same size and temperature as a mouse.

are lined with nerve cells sensitive to infrared radiation. These pits are like a pair of "heat-ray eyes." With them, the snake can "see" a mouse or any other warm creature, even on an absolutely pitch-dark night.

Each of these "heat-ray eyes" contains 150,000 heat-sensitive nerve cells. By contrast, a man has only about twenty heat receptors per square inch of skin, so that his awareness of infrared rays is far inferior to that of the snake. The information the snake receives through its heat receptors allows it to judge the warmth and approximate size of objects. The image it forms is apparently a fairly vague one, however, since snakes, when blindfolded, have been known to strike at light bulbs of roughly the same size and temperature as a mouse.

The pit vipers are not the only creatures to hunt by infrared rays. Mosquitoes and bedbugs can also find their victims by following heat rays to their source. Men, too, employ infrared rays for a specialized kind of night hunting. Of course, humans do not have "heat-ray eyes"; but human ingenuity has invented infrared devices that make it possible to locate objects in total darkness. A special infrared lamp is used to "illuminate" a landscape with infrared rays. This illumination can be viewed only through an infrared telescope. Without the telescope, the darkness is unchanged. Infrared telescopes, sometimes called snooperscopes, are especially useful for military purposes.

Man's uses for infrared radiation extend also into many non-military fields. Medicine, photography, cooking, and various industries all employ radiant heat. Doctors prescribe treatment with an infrared lamp for patients suffering from arthritis or muscular strain. The heat rays easily penetrate the skin, bringing soothing warmth to the aching muscles. Cooks find infrared ovens very efficient, because the heat passes quickly and thoroughly through the food.

Infrared photography is used mainly in darkness and fog. An infrared lamp is directed on a darkened scene, and the result is photographed with infrared-sensitive film. Many aerial photographs are taken with infrared film, which works well through clouds or mist.

Fighting forest fires with an airborne infrared scanner: it is used to locate the exact area of a huge fire. The naked eye can see only masses of smoke. The scanner can also be used at night—when even the smoke wouldn't be seen—and it can detect small fires before they are noticeable.

Cold Light

reflecting layer

scale

The lights of lantern fish might be yellow, blue or green. These light organs (above) are arranged in rows along the sides of the body. Light generated by the central organ is reflected by the silvery layer that surrounds it and is magnified by the thickened part of the scale, which serves as a lens.

In Central and South America there lives an insect known as the railroad worm. It got its name from the fact that it lights up as it crawls, and looks like a miniature railroad train. There are eleven pairs of green lights along the worm's sides, and two red spots on its head. Strange as it may seem, the railroad worm really does produce light; and it is only one of many creatures that light up in the darkness like living stars. Different types of glowworms and fireflies are common in the temperate regions of Europe and North America, as well as in tropical countries. And this ability to produce light is not confined to insects. The sea is filled with luminous creatures—some on the surface, and many at depths of up to eight thousand feet.

Tiny luminous bacteria often exist in the millions near the sea's surface, creating a brilliant glow on the water. When people speak of the phosphorescence of the sea, they are usually referring to the light produced by these minute creatures.

Scientists are very interested in studying the light-producing ability of animals, because they have found that animals are far more efficient at producing light naturally than men are at creating artificial light. Most of the electrical energy that goes into an ordinary electric light bulb is wasted as heat, and only three or four per cent is actually converted into light. A fluorescent tube is somewhat more efficient, but still only ten per cent

Noctiluca produce a stream of color in the sea by day and a swarm of luminosity at night. One of these single-celled animals measures only about one-twenty-fifth of an inch across.

of the energy becomes light, and ninety per cent is wasted. By contrast, the firefly apparently does not waste any energy in heat. Its light is perfectly cold, and virtually a hundred per cent efficient. Biochemists hope eventually to be able to duplicate this process, which was devised by nature millions of years ago, and to create light as efficiently as the firefly does.

It is now known that bioluminescence, or the light produced by living creatures, is the result of a series of complex chemical reactions. An animal produces one chemical called luciferin and another called luciferase. Luciferin combines with oxygen, releasing energy in the form of light. Luciferase acts

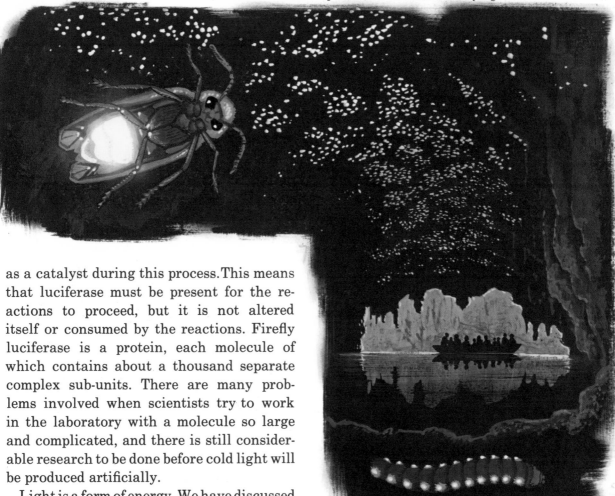

The adult firefly.

The larvae of fireflies in Waitomo cave in New Zealand, produce thousands of starry lights.

The larva of the beetle *Phrixothrix* is known as the railroad worm, because when lit up it looks like a lighted passenger train. Like the glow of the firefly, these lights are produced chemically.

as a catalyst during this process. This means that luciferase must be present for the reactions to proceed, but it is not altered itself or consumed by the reactions. Firefly luciferase is a protein, each molecule of which contains about a thousand separate complex sub-units. There are many problems involved when scientists try to work in the laboratory with a molecule so large and complicated, and there is still considerable research to be done before cold light will be produced artificially.

Light is a form of energy. We have discussed how some animals produce light by means of an energy-releasing chemical reaction. Other processes are responsible for producing different kinds of luminescence, such as the glow emitted by luminous paints. Most modern luminous paints, including those used on instrument dials, contain radioactive materials. These materials decay slowly, releasing particles which "excite" certain compounds in the paint and cause them to give off energy in the form of light.

We normally think of light as something to see by, and if scientists can produce light as cold as the firefly's, it will probably be used for lighting lamps of various kinds. Among animals, cold light has several different uses. Fireflies and other insects use light as a signal to attract members of the opposite sex. The male firefly flies through the air, flashing his light about every five-and-a-half seconds. The female sits patiently in the grass, waiting for a signal. When a female sees the light of a male, she responds, after an interval of two seconds, by flashing her own light. These signals may be exchanged many times before the male lands and mating begins.

Some fish apparently use their lights as searchlights. The lantern fish illuminate the water beneath them and seize upon any small marine animals that swim within range of the light. Certain deep-sea creatures use their lights as means of defense: various lantern fish and deep-sea shrimp can even "explode" with light, blinding their enemies with the flash.

Like the bird's oiled feathers, man's waterproof materials are treated with a water repellent. Thus, water is not soaked up, but stays on the surface.

Waterproofing

Everyone knows the advantages of wearing a raincoat in the rain. A good raincoat never gets wet all the way through because it "repels" water. This means that water is not soaked up by the fabric, but stays on the surface of the garment. Special water-repellent fabrics, such as those used for raincoats, are manufactured in several different ways. They may be coated with synthetic resins, oils, waxes, or metallic compounds that repel water without making the material stiff or heavy. Sometimes the fibers are treated before they are woven into cloth. A water-repellent garment may need to be re-treated after dry cleaning. Fabrics that are permanently waterproofed, however, will never need reprocessing, because the finish is baked on. They are heavier than water-repellent fabrics, and may develop cracks. This is why the raincoat you buy in a store will usually be water-repellent instead of permanently waterproofed.

Being dry is much more pleasant than being wet—and it's better for our health, too. Most animals also like to keep dry. Birds need some way of making their feathers water-repellent.

Most birds waterproof their feathers when they preen themselves. The beak is pressed against an oil gland at the base of the tail; then a thin coating of oil is put on the feathers by passing them through the beak.

If a duck, for example, were to become water-logged, it would not be able to fly. Studies of bird behavior indicate that most birds water-proof their feathers when they preen themselves. First the bird presses its beak against an oil gland at the base of its tail. Then it passes its feathers through the beak, transferring a thin coating of oil onto them. Not all birds have oil glands, and it is not known how birds without them manage to waterproof their feathers. Oil glands are especially well-developed in waterfowl. The young birds are not resistant to water, and their downy feathers easily become saturated when they swim. As they grow older, and learn to preen themselves, using the oil gland, their feathers gradually become more resistant to water.

Many animals do not have to make a special effort to waterproof their bodies. The water springtail is an insect that uses air as a waterproofing agent. It is covered with short hairs, set very close together. Without any action on the part of the springtail, these hairs help to create a "rain garment" for it. Air collects between the hairs and forms a protective layer that keeps the insect from becoming saturated. The water spring-tail lives on the surface of the water, feeding on weeds. Its raincoat of air keeps it dry, and also makes it so buoyant that it must work hard to force itself through the surface of the water in order to feed underneath.

Animals are not concerned with keeping only themselves dry. Many must make provision for eggs that are laid out in the open, on rocks or leaves. Female insects usually solve this problem by covering each egg with a kind of waterproof varnish. This is a thick, quick-drying liquid that protects the egg and also glues it firmly into place.

The water springtail, a tiny insect that lives on the surface of the water, is covered with short hairs, set very close together. Air collects between the hairs and forms a protective layer that keeps the insect from becoming saturated.

A swan enjoys the benefits of being a waterproofed water bird.

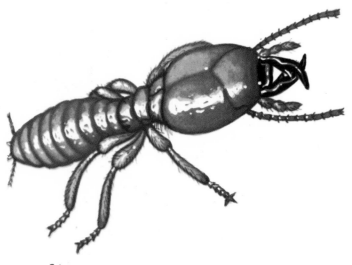

A termite mound is built to last. Made from mud and a cement manufactured from earth and vegetation mixed with the termites' own saliva and excreta, these mounds are practically indestructible. Below: the male termite.

Masonry

There are many thousands of animal architects which build intricate homes, nests, and nurseries. Some work with mud and clay, others with sticks and vegetable fiber, silk, paper, and other materials. Some of these builders are skilled "masons" which make their own cement. "Natural cement" is made by mixing together soil particles and other materials with the animal's own saliva. Man-made cement, which is usually compounded of clay or silicates, is mixed with water. Both the natural and the man-made products harden as they dry.

The southern European mason bee, which builds with pebbles and natural cement, is famed for its architecture. The mason bee is a solitary insect, preferring to live alone—unlike the social hive bees which live in large cooperating groups. The female mason bee builds a solid and secure nest for its offspring. The cement it makes becomes extremely hard and weather-resistant as it dries. The mason bee usually builds on the upper surface of a large stone, constructing between eight and twelve upright cells. These are composed of cement, with tiny pebbles embedded in the walls for extra strength. The inner surfaces of the cells are plastered with a smooth cement layer. The cells are then filled with honey, and the bee lays an egg on the top of each. This work is long and difficult; each cell takes about two days to build and fill with honey. And even when this task is finished, the mass of completed cells must still be enclosed by a thick, dome-shaped layer of masonry. When it is finally ready, the nest is about the size of half an orange.

The potter wasp is another solitary insect, and is so named because of its skillful nest-building. Like the common mud dauber wasps, which build their nests in crevices and even under pieces of furniture, the potter wasp works with mud. Some potter wasps have been observed using their own cement, but most employ mud for building. This wasp is really an artist in mud, creating miniature

The nest of the paper wasp is a complex of cells made of wood pulp. The wasps create this durable material by chewing wood and mixing it with saliva.

The potter wasp builds a tiny clay pot and fastens it to a plant. The female lays a single egg in this nest and then she fills it with paralyzed caterpillars—the future larva's larder.

globe-shaped vases, sometimes as small as half an inch in diameter. Each of these little vases is stocked with a supply of paralyzed caterpillars and contains a single egg. The wasp works for three to four hours to build and stock one of these vases, and finally completes the job by sealing the opening at the top.

The cement constructions of insects range from the very small and delicate vases of the potter wasp to the huge, rock-hard mounds of the termite. Termites are social insects, and the nests they build may have a million inhabitants. They work with mud and a

cement manufactured from earth and vegetation mixed with their own saliva and excreta. Termite mounds vary in size and shape, some looking like towers, others like mud huts. They may be as much as twenty feet high, and sometimes they are so hard that they cannot be entirely destroyed without the use of explosives.

Insects are not the only workers in cement. Some birds build amazingly strong nests from a mixture of earth or sand and other substances. The South American ovenbird uses sand and cow dung to construct a hollow nest that looks like a primitive baker's oven.

The rust-colored ovenbird of South America builds a nest of clay strengthened with grass. The nests, which look like ovens, are built in the winter when the rains have softened the clay.

Borers and Tunnelers

If you think back to when you were younger, you may remember spending hours digging in the earth or the sand. Even if you didn't have a shovel, digging was great fun; but if you did have one, you could shift far more soil in a much shorter time than you could without it. The human hand is a less efficient digging instrument than a spade or shovel. This is not a serious limitation, since men, although not adapted for a life of burrowing, can invent tools to assist them in digging holes. Animals —with few exceptions—do not use tools, and

The woodpecker penetrates the bark of trees with its beak in order to find the insects that live in the wood. Its skull is toughened to withstand the shock of drilling.

Above: Long, strong claws make it possible for badgers to dig vast underground systems to live in.

must live their lives within the limitations of their natural equipment. So it is not surprising to find that animals that do a great deal of digging are equipped with natural shovels. Similarly, animals which bore their way into earth, sand or wood can do this because they possess natural drills.

An animal like the mole, which spends most of its time underground, needs strong shovels for its work. Moles excavate for themselves a central living space called a fortress, from which tunnels radiate outward in all directions. They dig with their powerful limbs, which are flat and shovel-like. Their sharp claws are useful for breaking up

A mole can tunnel up to fifteen feet an hour, using the powerful claws of its front paws as digging tools.

hard-packed earth, and they use them much as you might use the point of a spade to loosen the soil before digging a hole.

Other mammals besides the mole have limbs adapted for digging. The badger's long claws and powerful paws allow it to dig extensive underground burrows. Shovel-like limbs are also found among insects, especially beetles such as the scarab beetle, the famous beetle which the Egyptians regarded as sacred. Another insect, the mole cricket, is an expert burrower whose flattened forelegs resemble the mole's "shovels."

Animals that bore their way through hard materials have specialized equipment, just as the diggers and tunnelers do. Some snail-like shellfish use their entire bodies as drills, twisting themselves downward into the sand. Often an animal uses a specially adapted mouth or beak for drilling a hole. The mouthparts of the snout beetle (also called the acorn weevil) form a long, slender drill strong enough to bore through an acorn. The snout beetle drills under the acorn shell to lay an egg inside the nut and provide the young beetle with a safe nursery stocked with its favorite food.

The woodpecker uses its beak like a chisel to penetrate deep beneath the bark of trees. It does this in order to find food, for it eats wood-boring insects that live in tunnels in the trunks of trees. After the woodpecker has opened a hole into the interior of the tree, it uses its narrow, flexible tongue to probe the tiny holes where its prey is living.

One of the best animal drillers has its drill, not at the front, but at the rear of its body. The ichneumon fly, like the wood-pecker, bores into trees to reach wood-boring grubs. The ichneumon fly, however, does this to lay its eggs on the bodies of the grubs, and its drill is a modification of its ovipositor, or egg-laying apparatus. With its long and slender drill, this delicate insect can drill one-and-a-quarter inches into solid timber in less than twenty minutes.

Right: Men have invented tools to assist in digging. A pneumatic drill can bore through solid cement.

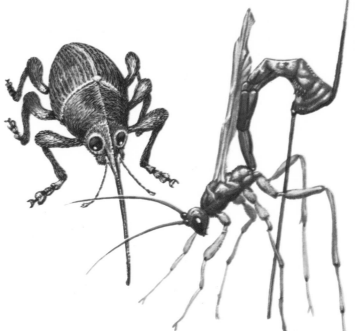

The female snout beetle (above, left) drills a hole in an acorn and then turns around to drop an egg into it. The drilling ovipositor of the ichneumon fly, or ichneumon wasp (right), can be as long as six inches. Its main use is to deposit eggs in the body of another insect, but one type of ichneumon uses this tool to bore through a couple of inches of solid wood first—and then to implant its egg in a grub living inside the tree trunk.

This razor shell, with its muscular foot extended, is about to burrow into the sand. One of many burrowing mollusks, the razor shell can dig to a depth of two or three feet.

Dams

In the state of Montana, in the northwestern part of the United States, is a dam 2,140 feet long, 12 feet high, and more than 15 feet thick. Built entirely of wood, mud and stone, the dam is a record-breaking feat of animal engineering. It is the largest beaver dam in the world. Most beavers build dams considerably smaller than this one, averaging four or five feet in height and perhaps several hundred feet in length. But even the average dam is a remarkable construction, able to withstand a tremendous amount of pressure from the water it is holding back.

Beavers build their dams across rivers. The purpose of a dam is to create a pool or lake of deep water, in which a large wooden house is constructed. This house, which is called a lodge, consists of a room above water level, with one or more entrances underwater. It is important to the beaver that the lodge be built in deep water, so that there is no possibility of the water's freezing solid during the winter, and blocking the underwater entrances. The beaver also stores its winter supply of food—logs and small branches—in the water near the lodge, and the water level must be sufficient to cover this store completely. When the surface of the lake freezes over, the beaver is in an ideal position, for both the beaver and its larder

Beavers are not only expert engineers; they are also good woodsmen. A beaver gnaws at a tree until it falls, then strips away the branches and cuts the trunk into manageable sections.

are absolutely secure from outside interference. The beaver can reach its storehouse by swimming under the ice, and none of its enemies, not even the fierce wolverines, can penetrate the strong walls of the lodge.

The beaver's chief building material is wood. It obtains this by felling trees, using its strong incisor teeth to gnaw straight through the trunks. Beavers often cooperate in felling trees, and some observers say that a group of them can gnaw through a tree trunk four feet around in about twenty minutes.

Hundreds of branches are plastered together with mud to form a dam that will create a pool of deep water. Then a lodge is built in the pool, with a room above water level and one or more underwater entrances. There is also a small underwater stockpile of logs and

small branches that will be the winter food supply for the young when the lake freezes over; older beavers eat very little in winter, for they live on their fat.

Dam building and repairing is so instinctive to beavers that they have been known to "repair" man-made concrete dams with sticks and mud.

Men build dams in order to control the natural water supply, in order to generate hydroelectric power, and sometimes simply to create an artificial lake for recreation.

Once a tree has fallen, the beavers strip away the branches and cut the trunk into manageable sections, about five feet in length. The wood is all floated downstream to the chosen site, and there the first branches are firmly anchored in place. Many hundreds of branches may be used in building a dam, and these are all carefully piled in layers and plastered together with mud to form a solid structure. Sometimes the beavers cut down all the useable trees surrounding the lake. When this happens, they build canals running outward from the lake for a hundred feet or more, which they use to float distant timber to the dam site.

It has been said by some engineering experts that the beaver produces a better dam than any man could, if he were to use the same materials. Human engineers make no attempt to duplicate the beaver's feats, however, and modern dams are usually constructed of earth, stone or concrete. Dams serve many purposes, including water storage, flood control, irrigation and the provision of power for generating stations.

Mobile Homes

Snails carry their homes around on their backs. They have been known to retreat into their shells for years at a time.

Most people live in homes that are firmly affixed to one spot. They may be huge apartment houses or small private residences, mud-walled huts or houses on stilts, but they are alike in that they are not easily moved. For some people who like to wander, however, a permanent dwelling is a handicap. They prefer a mobile home, one that they can live in and take along with them on their travels. Tents are conveniently portable, and for many centuries they have been a favorite form of shelter for nomadic tribesmen. Tents are also frequently used in military operations, and on ordinary camping trips. Other types of mobile homes, such as trailers or houseboats, are roomier and more comfortable to live in than a canvas tent. During

the past thirty years, trailers have become very popular, especially for long family vacations.

Certain animals also share the advantages of living in a mobile home. The snail, which carries its house around on its back, manufactures for itself a durable shelter exactly the right size. As the snail grows, it adds to its shell, so that it never needs to go looking for larger quarters. A snail does not shed or exchange its shell; it simply goes on enlarging it. The shell is composed of a limelike substance secreted by a fold of skin called the mantle. The mantle completely lines the shell and surrounds the snail's body. Secretions flow from the interior margin of the mantle throughout the life of the snail,

The modern man-made mobile home is a compact trailer complete with every convenience. It can be hitched to a car and driven away.

The ancient nomadic way of life in the Sahara: home is a tent and anything else that might be loaded onto the back of a camel.

and the evenness of the flow determines the smoothness of the shell. An even flow produces a smooth, thin shell, while an uneven flow results in a ridged and fairly thick shell. The snail begins constructing its shell at the small, pointed end, and as it grows, it continuously lengthens and widens the shell, by adding further coils or whorls. Most snail shells are right-handed spirals, although a few twist naturally to the left. If you hold a snail shell with the opening downward, and look at it from above, you will find that nearly always the shell spirals clockwise from the tip to the opening. This is what is meant by a right-handed spiral.

A snail's shell is usually large enough for the animal to retreat within it completely.

When a mollusk dies, its shell often becomes another animal's home. The hermit crab, for instance, must have such a shell to protect its soft abdomen.

Most marine snails not only have this home to retreat into, but they also have a door that they can use to shut out the world. This door is a horny plug called the operculum, which neatly seals off the opening of the shell.

The snail, as we have discussed, makes a life-long job of constructing its portable home. When the snail dies, this home is not wasted, however, for an empty snail shell can become a dwelling place for a variety of interesting creatures. The chief inhabitant of such shells is the hermit crab, which needs the hard shell to protect its soft abdomen. The crab curls itself into the spirals of an empty shell and holds onto it tightly, while it scuttles safely along the ocean floor.

This diagram shows how neatly the snail fits in its shell: (a) the head, (b) the foot, (c) the visceral mass containing internal organs.

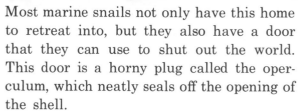

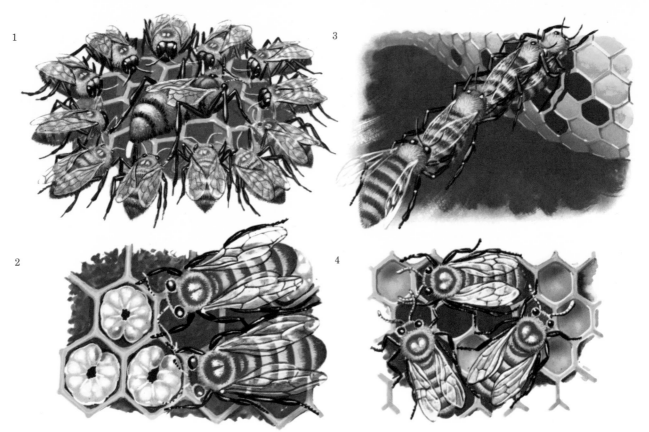

Communities

What will you do when you grow up? Be a doctor, or a dancer? Keep a zoo? Perhaps you feel absolutely certain of what you want to do; perhaps you really have no idea at all. But, being human and living in a modern society, you will find many different careers open to you. If you were a bee or an ant, or any other of the "social insects," you would have no choice about what to do with your life. Your job, your position in society, and even your sex would be regulated to suit the needs of the community.

"Social insects" are those that live together in large cooperating groups with members of their own species. In such a community, the members are entirely dependent upon one another, so much so that a social insect that is isolated from its fellows will quickly die. The main social insects are certain species of bees, ants, wasps and termites. Men have observed these insects, especially the bees, for centuries. They have found that the insect communities, which existed long before human ones, are very highly organized and

A hive of honeybees is one of nature's most efficient communities. Every activity of every bee is directed toward the bee-society as a whole. Some things that go on inside a hive:
(1) The queen bee, attended by workers, lays her eggs in an empty comb. The workers feed her with a special food produced by glands in their heads; only the queen is given this food, and it helps her lay up to 1,500 eggs in a day.
(2) For part of their lives worker bees are nurses, producing food and feeding it to the larvae.
(3) Worker bees become engineers in order to build the wax cells of the comb. To begin a comb, they hang in a string, one below the other, while wax is secreted from their abdomens.
(4) Worker bees store the nectar that the field bees have brought in from flowers. Later in their lives these same workers will become field bees, who spend all their time collecting nectar.

exceedingly complex. Insect communities cooperate to carry out numerous tasks, such as the care of the young, the building of a nest or hive, the production of food and the protection of the entire community. They achieve all this by means of an apportionment of the work, which has reminded some observers of a busy modern factory.

Because of the complex way in which these communities function, we cannot be too specific when comparing them to human institutions. The social insect does not have

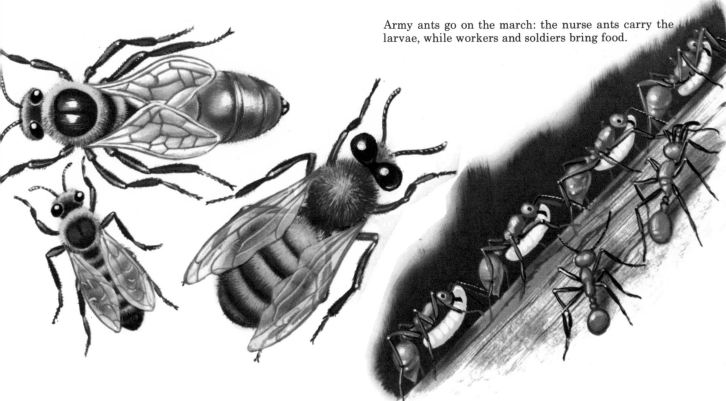

Army ants go on the march: the nurse ants carry the larvae, while workers and soldiers bring food.

What sort of life a bee leads depends on whether it is a queen, a worker or a drone. The queen (top) is the head of the community, and the only female that lays eggs. The drones (right) are males whose sole function is to mate with the queen. The workers are sterile females who do all the work of the hive.

Ants, like bees and termites, are "social insects"—that is, they live in large cooperating groups. The ants' nest is their communal home, and the center of all activity.

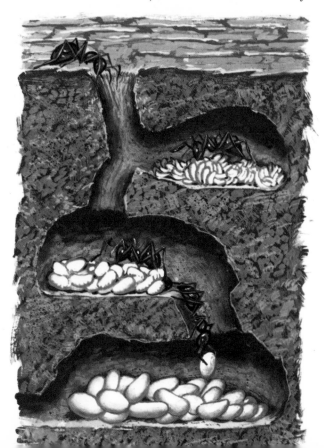

the independence or the freedom of a human being. It cannot be a hermit—it *must* join with its fellows, in order to survive. Also, as we have seen, the individual in an insect community has no free will. A honeybee, for example, may be a queen, a worker or a drone. If it is a queen, it is the head of a community or hive. It is a fertile female, whose job is to lay eggs; and this job is all that the queen does, laying perhaps 1,500 eggs in a day. A worker bee is a sterile female that does the work of the hive. A drone is a male bee that does not work. Its sole function is to mate with a young queen when a new community is being formed. Whether a honeybee is a queen, a worker or a drone, it plays its part automatically in the life of the community, rather like a small cog in a very large and complicated piece of machinery. In fact, the insect community could well be compared to a giant machine, but one far more elaborate than any that man has ever constructed.

What nature devised in the evolution of the social insects is a community system that is far more logical and efficient than the human one. But because of its machine-like qualities, there are few people who would prefer to live in that type of society.

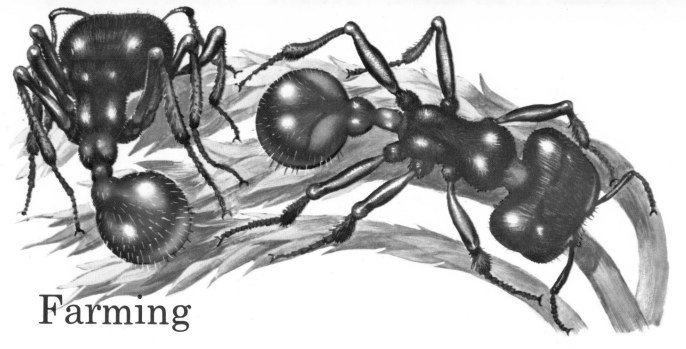

Farming

Man was first a hunter and a food-gatherer. With the passing of time, he learned to collect food and store it for future use. But it was not until man began farming that he developed any real "know-how" in this area. As a farmer, he used his intelligence to plan and to work together with other men to prevent food shortages. He became more settled, and began to learn how to live in a community. Thus, farming provided the foundation for our modern civilizations.

One might easily imagine that only man could have developed a procedure as advanced as farming. But in fact, as both storers of food and farmers, the ants began thousands of years before we did.

The authors of the Bible noticed the habits of certain food-storing ants, and wrote: "Go to the ant, thou sluggard; consider her ways and be wise; which . . . gathereth her food in the harvest." The ants they described were probably of the variety called *Messor*, or harvesting ants, which still inhabit the Mediterranean and Sahara regions. Harvesting ants gather grass seeds and store them in underground chambers until they are needed as food for the ant larvae. If the stored seeds become damp, the ants wait for a warm, dry day, and carefully place them out in the sun to dry. Thus, they not only gather and store their harvest, but they also act quite deliberately to preserve their stores.

Harvesting ants store food; they are not

Small harvesting ants (above) gather seeds to take back to the nest, where the grain will be husked by larger ants (below). Sometimes the grain stores germinate, and then the sprouting grain is thrown out of the nest to provide a future crop.

farmers. Other ants, however, actually do create and tend their own underground farms, described by naturalists as "mushroom gardens." These farming ants are a South American species called *Atta*, popularly known as parasol ants because they walk in long processions, each ant holding a piece of leaf over its head. The British naturalist Charles Waterton wrote of the parasol ants: "You will sometimes see a string of these ants a mile long, each carrying in its mouth to its nest a green leaf, the size of a sixpence. It is wonderful to observe the order in which they move, and with what pains and labour they surmount the obstructions of the path."

The ants carry their leaf sections back to the nest, where they use them as fungus beds —that is, they sow them with the spores of a particular type of fungus. This fungus grows rapidly to form a spongelike "mushroom garden," and the ants feed their larvae on its slender filaments. The mushroom gardens are constructed in underground chambers which may be several feet in length. Ventilation is carefully regulated by the opening and closing of air vents leading to the outside world. The principle is the same as that used by greenhouse gardeners, who open and close panes of glass to control the atmosphere in the greenhouse.

We have seen how fundamental the role of farming is in human activities. For the parasol ant, farming is essential for survival. When a young queen prepares to leave the nest, she always takes a supply of fungus with her; and one of her first tasks in forming a new nest is to create a fungus bed to provide food for the young ants as they hatch.

A combine harvester harvests and threshes grain at the same time—work that for centuries was done by hand.

The parasol ant is also known as the leaf-cutting ant because it slices up leaves for its underground "mushroom farm." Here a kind of fungus is grown for food.

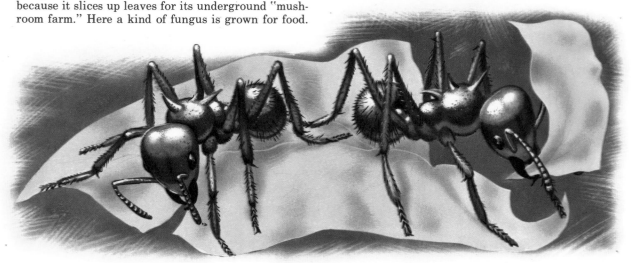

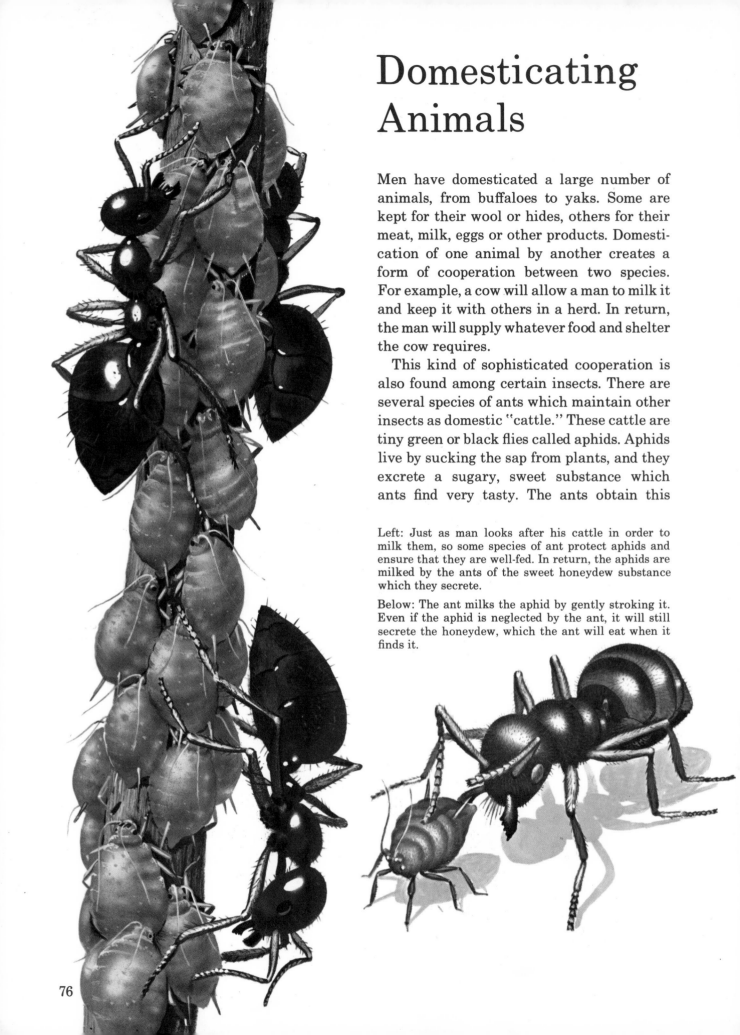

Domesticating Animals

Men have domesticated a large number of animals, from buffaloes to yaks. Some are kept for their wool or hides, others for their meat, milk, eggs or other products. Domestication of one animal by another creates a form of cooperation between two species. For example, a cow will allow a man to milk it and keep it with others in a herd. In return, the man will supply whatever food and shelter the cow requires.

This kind of sophisticated cooperation is also found among certain insects. There are several species of ants which maintain other insects as domestic "cattle." These cattle are tiny green or black flies called aphids. Aphids live by sucking the sap from plants, and they excrete a sugary, sweet substance which ants find very tasty. The ants obtain this

Left: Just as man looks after his cattle in order to milk them, so some species of ant protect aphids and ensure that they are well-fed. In return, the aphids are milked by the ants of the sweet honeydew substance which they secrete.

Below: The ant milks the aphid by gently stroking it. Even if the aphid is neglected by the ant, it will still secrete the honeydew, which the ant will eat when it finds it.

nectar by licking the bodies of the aphids—that is, by "milking" them. Some ants are content to milk aphids whenever they come across them. Other species, however, have become more systematic about obtaining the aphids' nectar. They maintain herds of aphid cattle, either on twigs or in stables of earth formed around the roots of plants. The ants are careful to keep the aphids adjacent to a good supply of food, and they will fight to protect them from attacks by enemies such as ladybird larvae. In the winter, the ants collect the eggs laid by female aphids, and bring these into their own nests while the cold weather lasts. When the young aphids hatch out in spring, they are put out to graze on their favorite food plants. Even then, the ants continue to bring their cattle back to the nest in the evenings, until the weather is warm enough for them to remain outside safely.

Man's domestication of animals is considered to be normal economic behavior. Slavery, however—the ownership by men of other men—is considered morally wrong. Slavery has a long history among mankind, but slavery was actually practiced first by ants. There are several varieties of slave-holding ants. The species most completely adapted to slave-holding is *Polyergus*, which cannot live without slaves. *Polyergus* workers have jaws that are well-suited for fighting, but not for feeding. They are wholly incapable of feeding themselves, and must capture slaves and be fed by them to survive. *Polyergus* soldiers form slave-raiding parties during the hottest part of the afternoon. They march in great columns, some eight inches wide, to ravage the nests of a peaceful species of ant, the *Formica fusca*. *Fusca* attempt to defend themselves, but are almost always defeated. The victorious *Polyergus* carry off the developing pupae of their victims. When the pupae emerge as adults from their period of metamorphosis, they are made to work as slaves for their *Polyergus* masters.

Right: Like sheepdogs, dairy ants herd and protect honey-giving tree hoppers.

Below: The slave society of the ant world. The pupae of the peaceful *Formica fusca* ants are carried away by the fierce marauders of the *Polyergus* army to become their future slaves.

The cleaner shrimp frequently takes a sea anemone as a neighbor, then attracts other fish by waving its antennae. Various species of marine life, including lobsters and eels, come to be cleaned of their parasites.

Partnership

Human society is built upon partnership and exchange. Just about everything we do depends on cooperation with other people. A similar situation exists in the animal world, where some creatures depend on others to do things for them that they cannot manage to do for themselves.

Some fish live by cleaning others. They establish themselves in a certain area, and set up a "cleaning station," where other fish come to have parasites removed from their bodies, and their mouth and gills thoroughly cleaned. The cleaner lives on the parasites, dead tissues and food particles that he removes from his "customer." Cleaner and customer (or host, to put it in more scientific language) thus form a temporary partnership that benefits them both. This type of mutually beneficial arrangement is called symbiosis, which means "living together."

There are about thirty known varieties of cleaner fishes and six species of cleaner shrimps. One such shrimp that has been studied very closely by marine biologists is the Pederson shrimp. This shrimp usually lives in a hole which it shares with an animal called a sea anemone. When a fish swims near the hole, the shrimp signals to it by waving its antennae and moving its body back and forth. If the fish needs a cleaning, it will stop close to the shrimp and allow it to climb onto its body and clean it from mouth to tail. The shrimp will even enter the fish's mouth, and walk lightly among its gills, removing

The oxpecker, or tickbird, can be seen on the backs of many different African animals. The bird will repay the hospitality of the animal by cleaning it of ticks, flies and lice, and will also warn it when danger approaches.

The Egyptian plover feeds on parasites found between the crocodile's scales, and will even enter its mouth to look for scraps of food when the crocodile basks with jaws agape.

any foreign matter that has lodged there. Cleaner shrimps such as this are never at a loss for customers, for once the fish in an area discover the location of the shrimp's hole they come automatically whenever they need to be cleaned. Sometimes several fish will arrive at once, and patiently await their turn.

Various cleaning arrangements exist between birds and larger animals. The tickbird removes parasites from the rhinoceros and other animals, and the Egyptian plover performs a similar service for the Nile crocodile. Sometimes these birds are useful to their hosts in other ways. For example, they may warn them of approaching danger by chattering excitedly. Such a warning could be especially helpful to a rhinoceros, for this huge beast has very poor eyesight.

Animal partnerships, like human ones, may serve many different purposes. One fascinating combination is the badger and the honeyguide. The honeyguide is a small bird that lives in forests. It is very partial to honeycomb, but it is not strong enough to break up a wild bees' nest by itself. So the honeyguide finds a badger and lures it to the nest by calling out repeatedly as it flies. The badger follows the honeyguide, and when they reach the bees' nest, the badger partly demolishes it. Then the badger eats its fill of honey, while the honeyguide feasts on the

honeycomb and on grubs that the badger does not care for.

Some very interesting associations are formed between hermit crabs and sea anemones. The hermit crab is a soft-bodied crab that makes its home in an abandoned snail shell. The sea anemone is a flowerlike animal with numerous stinging cells. Sea anemones attach themselves to the shells where hermit crabs live. Their stinging cells help to protect the crabs from enemies, while the sea anemone has the advantage of being carried around as the crab moves to new feeding grounds.

A wrasse inside the jaws of a barracuda. Cleaner fish are very thorough, removing bacteria, fungi and parasites from the bodies of larger fish, and even swimming inside their mouths and their gill chambers to complete the job. The cleaner fish gets a good meal out of it, and the larger fish, having benefitted from the attention, will let the cleaner fish depart unharmed when it has finished.

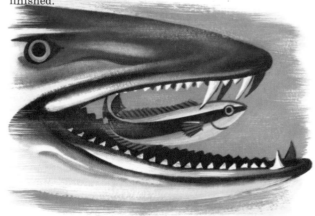

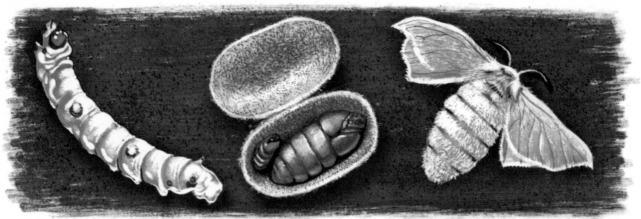

Chemical Fibers

The cocoon of the silkworm is made of a single thread of silk which is about 1,000 yards long.

Many insects could be described accurately as "manufacturers of fine silk fibers." They possess special silk-producing glands which enable them to manufacture delicate, gossamer-like threads. The location of these glands varies among different types of insects. In some insects, the glands lie behind the mouth, while in others they are linked with the excretory system. However, despite these differences in "apparatus," the method of silk production is basically the same among all insects and spiders. The silk-producing glands secrete a sticky substance which is ejected through a tiny opening called a spinneret. This substance solidifies upon coming into contact with the air, and the result is a continuous filament of silk.

Insects use their silk fibers to build shelters of various kinds. The most common type of silken shelter is the cocoon. Cocoons are structures built by caterpillars and some other larvae (young insects) to protect themselves during their period of change, or metamorphosis, into adult form. As the larva spins its cocoon, it moves its body around so as to enclose itself in a sealed chamber composed of hundreds of feet of silken fiber which hardens in the air.

Men have succeeded in obtaining this natural silk for commercial purposes by unraveling the cocoons of several varieties of moth. The most valuable silk is that yielded by the cocoons of the silkworm moth (*Bombyx mori*). Silkworm moths have been

Mussels attach themselves to rocks by means of byssus threads. These threads are made of protein and are strong enough to be woven into cloth.

The byssus threads of the mussel are made by the foot and are attached to it. In this diagram of the inside of a mussel, the foot is extended.

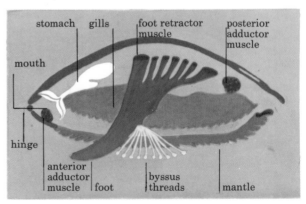

prized as manufacturers of silk for about 4,000 years. There is a legend that a young Chinese empress, after watching a silkworm spin its cocoon, dipped the cocoon into a cup of tea, and found to her delight that she could easily unwind the softened thread. Silk production remained a closely guarded secret of the Chinese for many centuries: anyone who revealed to a foreigner the true origin of silk fibers could be put to death. It was not until A.D. 550 that the first silkworms were smuggled into the Western world, and the European silk industry began.

Silk is only one of a number of natural fibers used in the manufacture of textiles. But man does more than adapt natural fibers to suit his needs. He has learned to rival nature's creations, and to produce, by chemical means, fibers which are entirely artificial.

Man-made fibers are among the most revolutionary of all synthetic products. All man-made fibers are created from huge molecules called polymers. The chemistry of synthetic fibers is extremely complex, but the physical processes by which continuous threads are produced are somewhat similar to those employed by insects and spiders. Four basic spinning methods are used, all of them involving the forcing of a sticky fluid through a small opening called a spinneret. After the fluid leaves the spinneret, it is passed through either a liquid or a gas which acts upon it to produce a continuous solid filament. In the case of nylon, probably the best-known of all man-made fibers, a heated "melt" of the polymer is solidified by a stream of cold gas—a process known as melt spinning. The final form of the synthetic fiber is largely dependent upon the shape of the spinneret.

The use of the spinneret was discovered in 1842 by an English weaver, Louis Schwabe, who forced molten glass through tiny openings to produce an unsuccessful version of fiberglass. We cannot help but wonder how much earlier this discovery might have been made if only men had paid closer attention to the silkworm at work.

Spider silk is spun by the spinnerets near the tip of the spider's abdomen. The silk coagulates as it comes out and becomes strong as the spider pulls on it. When the web is complete, it functions as a trap for insects—the spider's food.

Man-made fibers are created by a process similar to that used by insects and spiders: a fluid is forced through a small spinneret, then a liquid or gas acts on the fluid to produce a continuous filament.

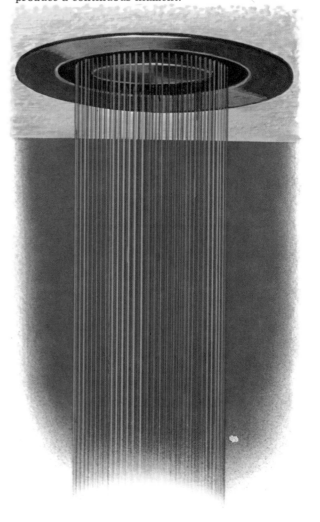

Weaving and Sewing

If men had not invented ways of weaving cloth and stitching materials together, we would still be draping animal skins over our bodies. Considering the widespread use of woven fabrics and rugs, and especially of garments woven of wool, linen, cotton and silk, we can see that weaving plays an important role in our lives. Sewing has even more varied uses, from the making of soft toys to the manufacture of seats for automobiles.

In the animal world, certain types of birds and insects are skilled weavers or tailors. They use their talents to make protective shelters for themselves. Perhaps the most dexterous of all nest-builders are the tropical weaverbirds. The weaverbirds are very neat workers, producing round nests carefully woven of plant fibers. They tie their nests to the branches of trees, using many interesting knots and ties. The sociable weavers build a large communal nest containing many individual chambers. There are other birds, as well, who weave nests, that of the African penduline titmouse being especially finely woven. The titmouse weaves a pouchlike nest, shaped like a large teardrop, with a short entrance tunnel along one side. At the opening to the tunnel it constructs a protective flap to discourage invaders.

A bird which actually sews is called the tailorbird. This bird builds a soft nest of stems, wool and down, which it protects by cradling it between two or more large leaves. Using thread, which it steals from spiders, or the cocoons of moths, or even human beings, the tailorbird delicately sews the leaves together. It punches holes in the leaves with its beak, ties knots on the ends of the threads, draws the threads through the holes, and then pulls them tight.

There are many different weavers among insects. Some caterpillars use the fine silk they secrete to weave nests in which they spend the early stages of their lives. The tent caterpillars build nests large enough to

The tailorbird's nest is made of leaves that it stitches together to form a pouch.

A Navaho Indian woman weaves a blanket of different-colored yarns. The basic act of weaving—crossing threads above and below one another—is also used by the weaverbird and by modern mechanized looms.

shelter perhaps 250 members of a brood throughout the winter. They settle on the branches of a tree or shrub, pull a number of leaves close together, and cover these with a layer of woven silk. This layer insulates the colony, by keeping in the warmth of the insects' bodies, and keeping out the cold.

The tent caterpillars remain in their nest all winter. In the spring, they emerge and split up into smaller groups. Each group then weaves a separate tent; these summer tents are more open, and thus less heavily insulated, than the winter ones.

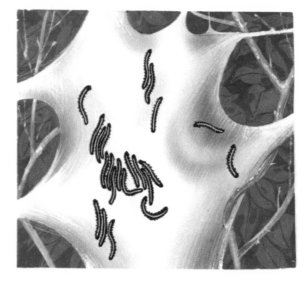

Above: Tent caterpillars weave tents from their silk secretions. In winter these tents are made big enough to shelter an entire colony of as many as 250 caterpillars.

There are several different species of weaverbirds, and each weaves a different type of nest. The weaving is done by threading, looping and knotting strips of flexible material, such as leaves or grass. Each new strip is held down with the foot while the free end is passed through the strips that are already in place.

Most remarkable among insect craftsmen is the weaver ant. This ant is one of the very few tool-using creatures in the world. Weaver ants build their nests in trees by joining leaf-edges together. First, several worker ants form a line along one leaf. They then seize the edge of a second leaf, and pull the two together. Another worker approaches, holding in her jaws a larva, or young ant, which secretes a continuous silk thread. While the workers hold the leaves together, the weaver uses the young ant as a tool, moving it back and forth between the leaf edges until they are held firmly together by a network of silken threads.

Air Conditioning

There are certain varieties of insects that live together in large cooperating societies. Among the major varieties are ants, bees and termites. The activities of these "social insects," as they are called, are discussed in detail in an earlier chapter. Here we will concentrate on just one of their many fascinating activities—the air conditioning of their nests or hives.

The air conditioning units we see in shops and houses regulate the temperature, humidity and air movement in enclosed spaces. Of all social insects, the bees come closest to achieving the kind of air conditioning produced by such man-made units, but the other social insects are also quite adept at controlling the temperature of their environments. The simplest system is one used by the ants to reheat and reactivate their nests after their winter's sleep. Hibernating ants crowd together in a large chamber located several feet underground. Within this hibernation chamber the temperature remains constant at about 50° Fahrenheit. The ants are safe from frost, but they are also buried so deep that the warmth of the spring sun can barely penetrate their nest. Somehow, the chamber must be warmed, so that the sleeping ants will awaken and resume their normal activities. This warming process is accom-

Some worker bees, stationed at the hive entrance, fan their wings vigorously to drive air inward and cool the hive.

plished, very gradually, by certain worker ants that act as "thermic messengers." These messengers are not as sensitive to cold as the majority of ants in the nest, and they do not hibernate. Instead, they spend the winter wandering between the hibernation chamber and the surface of the ant hill. As spring approaches, the messengers venture into the open air, where they absorb the warmth of the sun. Then, when they return to the hibernation chamber, they bring into it this extra warmth. Other ants awaken and go out, and the process continues until the

Man has learned how to regulate the indoor temperature, humidity and movement of air to suit his comfort —whatever the weather.

This cross-section of a termite mound shows the air vents which allow air to circulate throughout the nest. These vents pass so near to the crust of the nest that oxygen is taken in and carbon dioxide expelled through the wall.

entire colony is awake and active again.

Termites regulate the temperature in their gigantic nests by means of dozens of ventilation shafts located within the walls. A termite nest may be up to twenty feet high. The walls are as hard as cement, and are heavily ridged. Within the ridges are groups of vertical air vents. Hot air travels downward through these vents, cooling off along the way, and is released into a large underground vault. It then rises gradually through the various chambers of the nest. Termite workers are constantly engaged in altering the size of the air vents, according to the amount of sun striking the nest.

Honeybees employ various stratagems to maintain an even temperature in the hive. In hot weather, most of the worker bees leave the hive, to eliminate the heat generated by their presence. Several bees remain at the hive entrance, fanning their wings vigorously, to drive air inward. If necessary, other workers bring in water and carefully wet the entire surface of the honeycomb. As the water evaporates, it helps to cool the food supplies and the developing young to the required temperature of 95° Fahrenheit. In cold weather the bees reverse their strategy, and cluster together on the top of the comb to generate as much heat as possible.

Incubators

Mammals and birds—the warm-blooded creatures—maintain the temperature of their bodies at a fairly constant level. They must do this to survive, for if a warm-blooded animal grows too hot or too cold—even by a few degrees—it will become very ill, and perhaps die. An unborn bird or mammal, such as an embryo chick or a human baby in the womb, must also be kept by its parent at a suitable temperature. Embryos are even more sensitive to their surroundings than adult creatures, and must have an atmosphere of just the right amount of heat, moisture and oxygen to develop properly.

Unborn birds develop inside eggs. There,

For the first few days after the egg has been laid, the male and female emperor penguins share the incubation duties. This is done by balancing the egg, which is covered with a fold of skin, on their feet. Later the male is solely responsible for keeping it warm until it hatches.

Below: A premature human baby in an incubator.

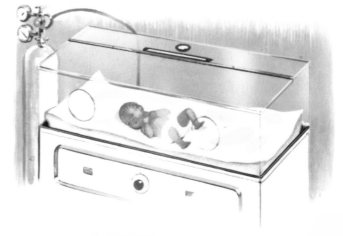

the humidity is constant, and oxygen is obtained through openings, or pores, in the shell. Heat is nearly always provided by one or the other of the parent birds, which incubates the eggs by sitting on them until the baby birds are ready to hatch. Most mammals develop inside their mother's body, where heat, moisture and oxygen supplies are automatically regulated to suit the embryo's needs.

Farmers often prevent hens and other fowl from incubating their eggs by removing the eggs from the nest before they hatch. This is done to induce the mother bird to lay more eggs, rather than continue to sit on those already laid. When fertilized eggs are removed, for the purpose of producing more young birds, farmers must incubate the eggs without actually sitting on them, as the mother hen does. They do this by using special devices called incubators.

In ancient times, incubators were mud-walled houses, heated by a continuously

is often called the incubator bird. The male incubator bird digs a hole in the ground some fifteen feet across and three to four feet deep. It fills this hole with leaves and grasses, and forms a depression in the top layer. This depression is used as an egg chamber. The eggs are laid in it, and the mound is covered with a two-foot layer of sandy soil. As the vegetable material decomposes, it produces heat which incubates the eggs. The male bird continually tests the temperature of the mound by thrusting its beak into the soil; according to what its "thermometer" registers, it will dig air vents or shift layers of sand in order to maintain the proper temperature. An incubator bird keeps its nest at almost exactly 92° Fahrenheit. Its measurements are so precise that a scientist who attempted to defeat it by heating and cooling the mound artificially found that he could not alter the temperature faster than the incubator bird could correct it.

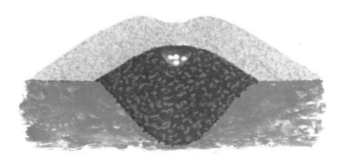

burning fire. Today they are complex pieces of apparatus, temperature-controlled by sensitive thermostats. Some incubators are used to hatch eggs, and some to grow bacteria. Others have been adapted to suit the needs of human embryos. A premature baby, born before it is ready for the outside world, may survive if he is placed in the controlled atmosphere of a specially designed incubator.

The problem of incubating eggs without sitting on them has not been solved only by men, but also by birds called mound-builders or megapodes. The most complicated incubation procedure among these birds is that of the Australian Mallee fowl, which

The Australian Mallee fowl constructs its own incubator in the ground (above, left), and constantly tests the temperature with its beak.

Below: An unborn chick develops inside the egg.

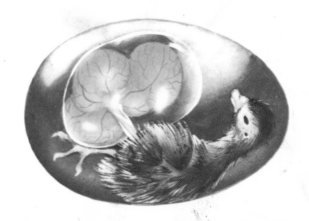

Curled up tightly in this comfortable position, the squirrel will hibernate through the winter and will not awaken until the temperature outside rises.

Hibernation and Hypothermia

During the winter months, severe cold, combined with a shortage of food, makes life difficult for many animals. Some of them solve the problems that winter poses in a very easy and natural way. They retire into some sheltered place, and there they fall into a deep, quiet sleep. Often their sleep lasts throughout the cold weather, until spring arrives. This period of sleep is known as hibernation.

A hibernating animal is not simply asleep in the ordinary sense. Its breathing and heartbeat are very much slower than normal. In fact, its entire metabolism slows down so drastically that the animal can survive without food for months at a time, living on the reserves of fat stored in its body. Accompanying all these changes is a great reduction in body temperature. Sometimes the temperature of the animal's body drops to match that of its environment. The entire body may become stiff with cold. Even so, the animal's fat never freezes, and the hibernating creature never fails to awaken when the outside

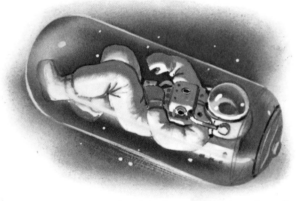

Scientists are investigating the possibilities of putting man into a state of hibernation so that very lengthy space journeys might be completed without need of food or exercise.

temperature rises to a more congenial level.

Most of the animals that hibernate are fairly small—for example, groundhogs, chipmunks, frogs, tortoises and bats. Men do not hibernate; they have other ways of dealing with the cold, and furthermore, their bodies do not enter naturally into a state of hibernation. Nevertheless, the process of hibernation in animals is of interest both to medical scientists and to space engineers. These men are carefully studying nature's methods, in the hope of employing similar techniques for the benefit of mankind.

Medical science has already devised a procedure for inducing in patients a state that is very much like hibernation. The technique, known as hypothermia, is used to create anesthesia, or loss of sensation. Hypothermia is the uniform reduction of body temperature, from the normal 98.6° Fahrenheit to about 77° Fahrenheit. It is used in such difficult operations as open-heart surgery, and also in cases where it could be dangerous to use other forms of anesthetic on a patient. As the patient's temperature is lowered, he passes through a number of strange states. Below 94° Fahrenheit, he loses both sight and hearing. Below 85° Fahrenheit, the body's thermostat, or "heat control center," ceases to send messages to the blood vessels, sweat glands and other mechanisms that help to maintain the body's normal temperature. At this stage, the patient feels nothing. His pulse is down from the normal 70 to 75 beats per minute to about 40 beats per minute. Five degrees lower, at 80° Fahrenheit, the patient appears to be in a state of hibernation. At about 77° Fahrenheit, he is connected to an artificial respirator, and surgery begins. After the operation, the patient's body is carefully reheated. As his temperature rises, his body returns to normal, and he regains his sight and other senses.

A person under hypothermia "hibernates" for a number of hours. Scientists concerned with space travel have suggested that astronauts on long journeys could be frozen into a state of suspended animation for months or even years. This would solve a multitude of problems: a hibernating traveler would not need food or exercise, books, games or any other form of entertainment. So far, no techniques have been developed which would allow a human being to survive the lowering of his body temperature below the freezing point. Animals can survive this, however, and continued studies of the animal world may yet provide an answer to this problem.

The whippoorwill is a North American bird that hibernates because its diet consists mainly of insects, which become scarce in the winter.

There is a legend in America that on February 2 the woodchuck (also known as a groundhog) emerges from its burrow to test the weather: if it sees its shadow, it returns to sleep for another six weeks. But if it does not see its shadow, then spring has come. During hibernation, the woodchuck's temperature drops from around 100°F to around 50°F.

Below: Reptiles have very little control over their temperature, their body heat depending almost entirely on the outside temperature. An underground burrow is far warmer than the ground surface, so it makes a good place for the winter sleep.

The Hypodermic Sting

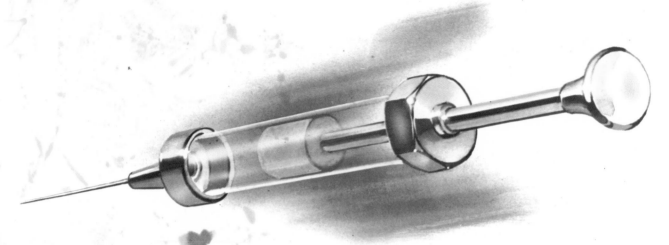

A small child, after paying a visit to the doctor, announced to her family, "I didn't like the doctor at all. He bit me." It had been her first experience of receiving an injection given with a hypodermic syringe. The hypodermic syringe, known to many people as "the needle," is used to administer drugs by injecting them directly into the tissues lying under the skin. A syringe has three basic parts: a cylindrical tube, which contains liquid; a disc-shaped piston, usually made of metal, which fits closely within the tube and moves up and down inside it; and a nozzle, through which liquid may be drawn up and ejected. The piston is connected to a rod which extends beyond the opposite end of the syringe from the nozzle. This rod allows the person using the syringe to control the movements of the piston within the tube. In the hypodermic syringe, the tube is made of glass, the piston and the rod are of metal, and the nozzle is a hollow, sharp-pointed metal needle, capable of piercing the skin. It is this sharp point that jabs or "bites" the patient when he is given a hypodermic injection.

All syringes work on the principle of suction. The piston is pushed down as far as it will go, driving air out of the tube. The tip of the nozzle is then placed beneath the surface of the liquid with which the tube is to be filled. The piston is drawn up, and atmospheric pressure forces the liquid up through the nozzle and into the tube. When

A hypodermic syringe has three basic parts: a cylindrical container, a piston that moves up and down inside it, and a hollow needle.

the tube is to be emptied, the piston is pressed down firmly, and the liquid is forcibly ejected through the nozzle.

Certain bees, wasps and other insects have their own version of a hypodermic syringe—

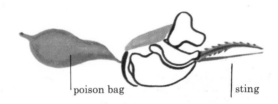

poison bag   sting

This section of a honeybee's sting shows the stylet sheath and one of the barbed lancets. When the bee stings, it often dies, for part of its abdomen is torn off. It is this part that contains the poison gland, which continues to pump poison into the wound after it has been torn away from the bee. Attempts to remove the sting only pump in more poison.

The honeybee.

the sting—which they use to injure and destroy their enemies. The construction of the sting differs from that of the hypodermic syringe, but the basic idea is the same, in that a liquid is forcibly ejected through a hollow, pointed tube. An insect uses its sting to inject a complex chemical poison beneath the skin or outer membrane of its victim. Only female insects have stings, because the

Stinging insects have a pouch at the base of the sting that contains poison. When the sting has penetrated the skin of the victim, muscular contractions of the poison bag force the poison into the wound.

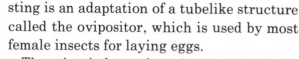

poison gland

sting

sting is an adaptation of a tubelike structure called the ovipositor, which is used by most female insects for laying eggs.

The sting is located at the very tip of the insect's abdomen or rear end. The poison is contained in a bag or pouch located at the base of the sting. This bag is filled by the action of certain glands which pour their secretions directly into it. The structure of the sting itself varies among different insects. In a honeybee it consists of three pointed needles, two of which are barbed. These are arranged so that they surround a hollow space like a canal. The thickest needle, which is called the stylet sheath, lies uppermost; the other two slide back and forth along miniature rails located on the lower edge of the stylet sheath. After the three needles have penetrated a victim's skin, muscular contractions of the poison bag force the liquid poison through the hollow canal and into the wound.

A hawk wasp stings a spider. Poison is injected beneath the outer membrane of the victim through the sting— which is located at the tip of the wasp's abdomen.

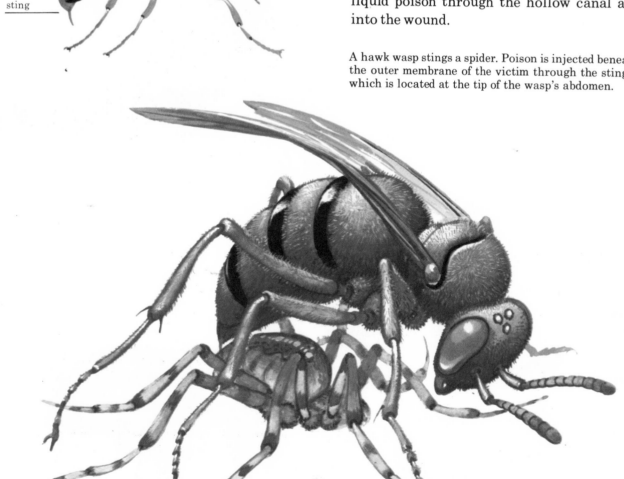

Electrical Batteries and Generators

Many people mistakenly assume that electricity is something found only "inside machines." But electricity exists throughout the natural world, and is the source of movement in all living things. Some forms of electricity are more spectacular than others. Lightning flashing across the sky is more exciting than the twitch of a muscle, but electricity is responsible for both.

Human beings may notice a crackle when they comb their hair or stroke the cat, but in general we are not very sensitive to electricity. We cannot, for instance, sense the direction in which an electric current flows— whereas a microscopic animal called the paramecium can detect it without fail. Tiny amounts of electricity are produced by cells in the human body, but man has no special organs which are sensitive to electricity, and has no particular "electrical sense." Such a sense does exist among various groups of fish. Some of these merely respond to electrical currents in the water, while others are equipped to generate their own electricity, which they use to learn what is going on around them.

One fish which explores the world by means of electricity is the African knife-fish. In fact, this fish could be described as a living electric battery. It has special electric organs producing electric pulses at the rate of 300 per second. The fish's head is positively charged and its tail is negatively charged. A weak

Above: The electric eel can discharge enough volts to stun a man. As many as 10,000 cells generate 550 volts.

The African knife-fish, like the eel, has a positively-charged head and a negatively-charged tail. An electric current flows between the two, creating an electrical field around the fish.

Diagram of an electricity-producing organ. Each "battery" is composed of electric plates, which are really altered, modified muscles.

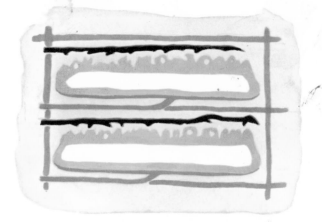

electric current flows between the two, creating an electrical field around the fish. The fish's "battery" is always connected because it lives in water, which is a good conductor of electricity. (A man-made battery, such as those used in transistor radios, contains two metal electrodes, one positive and one negative. When these are connected to a material that conducts electricity, an electric current begins to flow.)

The knife-fish puts its electrical field to practical use. All over the fish's body are minute organs sensitive to electricity, which register any disturbance in the electrical field around the fish. Thus it can sense the presence of obstacles in the water some three to six feet away.

There are other electric fish which can produce currents far stronger than the knife-fish. These fish use their electrical charges to shock other fish into unconsciousness before eating them. More than 2,000 years ago, the great Greek philosopher Aristotle observed the stunning powers of the torpedo ray. He wrote that the ray "narcotizes the creatures it wishes to catch, overpowering them by the strength of the shock which resides in its body."

The torpedo ray has two large organs, shaped like kidney beans, located on either side of its eyes. It lies in wait on the sea bed until a suitable prey comes within range of its paralyzing shocks. Then it stuns its victim with a charge of up to 220 volts.

The most dangerous of all electric fish is the electric eel, whose discharge is powerful enough to stun a man. An electric eel has between 6,000 and 10,000 separate generating cells which together yield a discharge of some 550 volts. Like the African knife-fish, the electric eel has a positively charged head and a negatively charged tail. Current flows around and through the eel, but, because of the presence of fatty tissue surrounding its essential organs, the eel does not electrocute itself.

Although, as we have said, man himself does not have a strong "electrical sense," he has discovered how to create electricity and

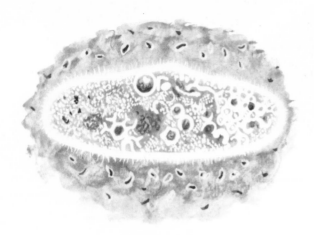

In a current of moderate strength, the one-celled paramecium swims toward the negative electrode. In a strong current, this microscopic animal swims toward the positive electrode.

The torpedo ray paralyzes its prey with a charge of up to 220 volts. Its electricity-producing organs are on either side of its eyes.

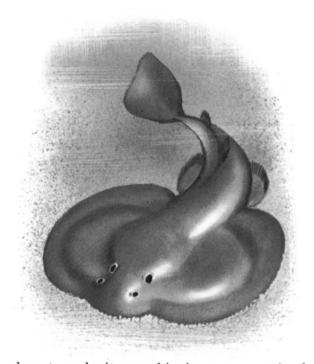

how to make it serve him in ways no animal ever could. As long ago as 600 B.C. men found that amber became charged when it was rubbed. (In fact, the word "electricity" is derived from the Greek word for amber.) Now, our everyday life depends largely on electricity. We use it to heat and light our homes, run our cars, trains and airplanes, bring us television pictures and radio sounds, cook our food and even warm our beds.

"When I'm playful . . . I scratch my head with the lightning and purr myself to sleep with the thunder." So wrote Mark Twain in his book *Life on the Mississippi*. The picture he conjures up is quite a fantastic one, especially since most people regard lightning and thunder with considerable respect. Lightning is one of the most awesome spectacles in nature. The sight of a fork of lightning splitting the sky has long been associated in men's minds with supernatural powers, and gods of thunder and lightning are mentioned in the mythologies of various nations. In actuality, a flash of lightning is simply an enormous electric spark visible in the sky. This spark may leap from one cloud to another, or from a cloud to the earth. It may also be confined within a single cloud.

When a thundercloud is formed, positive and negative electrical charges are produced. During a storm, the surfaces of the cloud become charged with electricity, the positive charges being carried toward the upper parts of the cloud, while the negative charges travel downward to the lower portion. This separation of charges is caused by collisions among ice pellets, droplets of water, and molecules of gas within the cloud. Heavy pellets of hail may become negatively charged, while lighter splinters of ice acquire a positive charge. As the heavy pellets fall downward, and the lighter splinters rise, the surfaces of the cloud become oppositely

A flash of lightning is really an enormous electric spark between a positively charged region and a negatively charged region of a thundercloud—or between one such region and the earth.

This diagram of a thundercloud shows how the surfaces of the cloud become charged with electricity during a storm. The positive charges (+) go toward the top of the cloud, while the negative charges (−) collect toward the bottom.

94

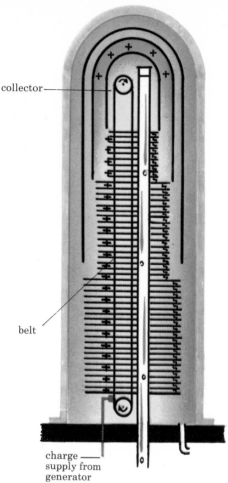

collector—

belt

charge —
supply from
generator

Right: The Van de Graaff generator is capable of producing artificial lightning. Thousands of volts, either negative or positive, collect at the top of the machine. When the voltage difference between this dome and the earth has become very great, it is possible to produce a spark of "lightning."

charged. Gradually, the electrical pressure, or voltage, between the positively and negatively-charged regions becomes so great that a spark is discharged across the gap between them, or between one such region and the earth. Considerable voltage is needed to create such a spark, as air is an excellent insulator (that is, it can stop the movement of an electric current). About one million volts are required to send electricity across a mile of air, and the voltage within a thundercloud may rise to one thousand million volts before a giant lightning flash is discharged.

It is no wonder, then, that men do not often refer to lightning as casually as Mark Twain did. However, although we cannot claim to be able to control nature's lightning, scientists can readily produce artificial lightning in the laboratory. They can do this by means of a machine called the Van de Graaff generator, which can generate voltages consisting of millions of volts. The Van de Graaff generator operates as follows: At the

bottom of the machine is an electric generator that produces an electric current of about 20,000 volts. This generator has a negative and a positive terminal. A series of metal spikes are attached to one or the other of these terminals, depending upon whether the scientists wish to collect negative or positive charges at the top of the machine. The spikes receive charges from the terminal and convey them to a moving belt made of insulating material. The belt carries the charges to a hollow copper dome at the top of the machine, and deposits them there. As the charges collect on the dome, the voltage difference between the dome and the earth grows until the machine is capable of producing a spark of artificial lightning. Usually the voltage is prevented from discharging in this manner, and is used instead to accelerate streams of similarly charged particles. These streams of particles are used in turn to bombard specific "target" atoms; this generator thus plays an important part in nuclear research.

Index

Figures in bold face refer to illustrations